AF413599

THE JOURNEY TO INFINITY

A TIME TRAVEL TALE

KANAK WASNIK | ARUN D I

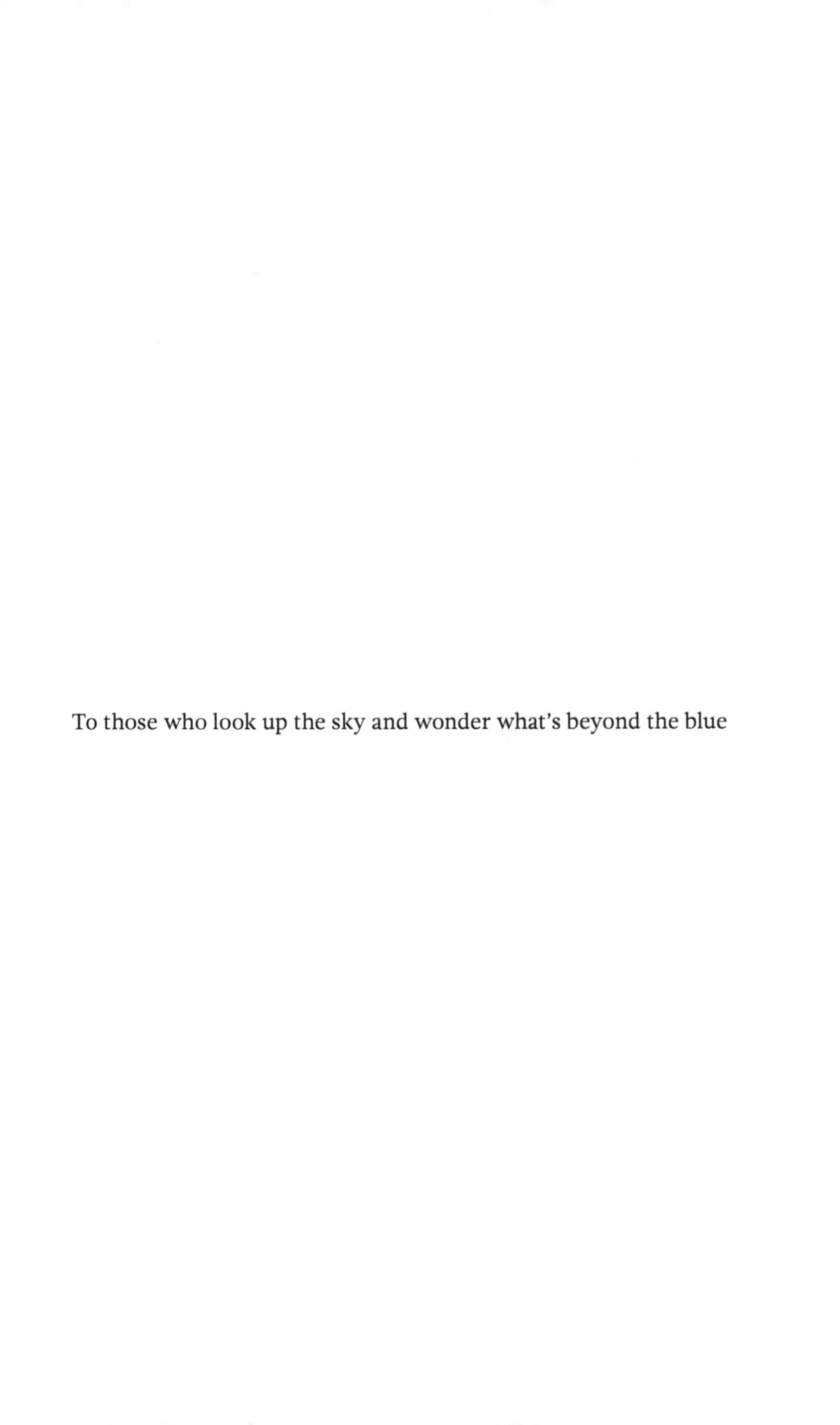

To those who look up the sky and wonder what's beyond the blue

Contents

Contents

About The Authors

Ms. Kanak Wasnik is a student of the Christ University Bangalore, pursuing her Bachelor of Science - Honours degree (Physics & Mathematics). She enjoys collaborating with researchers, particularly those exploring space science, with an open mind and unrestricted access to information. She strives to adapt and innovate, aiming to generate unexpected breakthroughs for the betterment of science and humanity. Kanak completed her schooling from Montfort school, Ashokwan, Nagpur, Maharashtra. Apart from being a science enthusiast, she's a pianist, artist and a traveller.

This book has evolved out of her association with Dr. Arun D I, in their quest to study about the deepest secrets of Space.

Dr. Arun D I is a scientist at the Vikram Sarabhai Space Centre, ISRO. He's working with composite materials for launch vehicles & spacecrafts of Indian Space Research Organization. He has authored many research publications, science articles, book chapters and various books in academic genres as well as literary works. Few books written by Arun are Shape Memory Materials (Science), Verdical (Novel-English), Paradoxical (Novel-English), Dnieper Nadikkippuram (Anthology - Malayalam), Bodhanam (Anthology - Malayalam), How I cured my hypnic jerk (Fiction - English), Lunaris (Science), Manushyanum Bahirakashavum (Science), Cycle muthal Rocket vare (Science), Chandrante Kadha (Science).

Apart from writing, Arun is interested in art, travelling and music.

-

Reach the authors at:
kanakwasnik@gmail.com / authormearun@gmail.com
+91 9049049938 / +91 9495277367

Preface

We all have waved at an aeroplane in the blue backdrop of the beautiful skies. We all have imagined of flying a plane.

Isn't it one of the happiest memories about childhood?

Why aren't we doing it as grown-ups?

May the term 'maturity' burden us to forget, forego such dreams and walk into the created reality!

What's reality?

Is it what we see around? Rather, is it what is shown around?

Debatable of course, in the multitudinal dimensions though.

As we struggle in the so called 'reality', the fantasies paves way to the variegated world beyond what we see!

Fantasy refers to a genre of imaginative fiction characterized by elements of magic, supernatural phenomena, mythical creatures, and fantastical worlds that exist outside the realm of ordinary reality. As we get on for a voyage to get away from reality, we can define it as 'imagination'.

Imagination is a term to be cultivated before introducing any unconscious cognition to the mind.

Presented as a narrative, this book is an account of our attempt to understand the universe, its vastness and to get humble in front of the scale with infinite dimensions. As we look forward, we receive light from events which happened in past at different galaxies. This means we're looking to future and watches the past - a beautiful paradox.

Each chapters of this book is titled with the 'time to reach the respective celestial objects', in the journey, at a speed of ONE LIGHT YEAR PER SECOND.

The book is written to address the curious questions of a teenager, the inquisitive mind of a researcher, to kindle the imaginations of a common man to appreciate the beauty of the cosmos and to feel humble.

Let's travel beyond what's seen and shown. Let's travel to past and future.

Let's travel in time.

-
Kanak / Arun

Acknowledgements

Thanks
    to our families,
    to everyone who taught us to ask questions,
    to those authors of various books who gave answers,
    to those beautiful dreams and fantasies,
    to Kavya, Padma and Aarav

Prologue

As I was walking past 'Pondy Bristo', Tavarekere - a neighborhood in Bangalore India, a motor-bike squeaked and went past at about an inch or less from me, almost killing my senses for a moment. I breathed again with a soliloquy 'Watda Fastt !'

'Fast' is a measure in the scale of moving or ability to move rapidly. Rather it's an indication of Speed of an object.

Speed can be defined as *'Ratio of the distance traveled by an object (regardless of its direction), to the time required to travel that distance'.*

As the scalar speed catches a direction, it becomes velocity. In this dynamic world, everything is moving. The air particles, clouds, aeroplanes, vehicles, tectonic plates, animals, birds, us humans, heart, blood, Earth, Moon, Sun, Galaxies and the Universe itself is moving.

As we look through the known objects and their speed,

A Leopard-tortoise walks a kilometer in one hour, while a Saharan silver ant walks 3.1 kilometer in an hour.

Eight time Olympic Gold medalist Usain St. Leo Bolt, the Jamaican sprinter ran into records with a speed of 44.72 km/h (12.42 m/s).

The Cheetah (scientific name: Acinonyx jubatus), a large cat and the fastest land animal runs at 130 km/h (36.1 m/s).

A Peregrine falcon can swoop faster than a cheetah at a speed of 300 km/h (83.3 m/s).

Sound waves can travel at speed of 1,236 km/h (343.3 m/s) in room temperature.

Our planet Earth spins on its axis at about 1,600 km/h (460 m/s).

'Dodamma', the Godfather of all large guns used by 'ROCKY BHAI' of KGF-2, in one of the most iconic scenes in Indian cinematic history, is an M1919 American Made Browning Machine Gun which has a muzzle speed of 3,070 km/h (853 m/s).

Moon orbits Earth at a speed of 3,683 km/h (1023.06 km/s).

NASA's X-43, an experimental unmanned hypersonic aircraft attained a top speed of 11,854 km/h (3292.78 m/s).

American Space Shuttle has registered speeds over 27,359 km/h (7,599.7 m/s), and the Apollo manned spacecraft traveled between the earth and the moon at speeds closer to 39,428 km/h (10952.2 m/s), thus making the men in these vehicles as the fastest humans.

Voyager 1, the space probe launched by NASA on September 5, 1977 to study the outer Solar System and the interstellar space beyond the Sun's heliosphere moves at a speed of 61,493.03 km/h (17,081.4 m/s).

During the 7 years of expedition in space, the Stardust spacecraft raced along at an average speed of 78,000 km/h (21,666.67 m/s).

Earth, in its orbit, revolves around the Sun at a rate of about 107,000 km/h (29722.23 km/s).

'Operation Plumbbob', a series of nuclear tests conducted by United States during the year 1957, at the Nevada Test Site has led to one of the fastest object shot into outerspace - a manhole cover. During one of the explosion, inside a hole covered with an iron cover, the iron manhole cover was launched at a speed of 2,01,168 km/h (55,880 m/s).

Nasa's Parker Solar Probe, as it continues its mission hurtles around our Sun, registers its speed of 6,35,266 km/h (1,76,462.78 m/s) as the fastest ever man-made object.

We know something faster than this, which covers the distance from Earth to Moon approximately in a second, that which covers distance between Earth and Sun in eight minutes.

Light!

The speed of light in vacuum is a universal physical constant which is 1079252848.79 km/h (or 299,792,458 m/s). Special theory of relativity considers this as upper limit for the speed at which conventional matter or energy can travel through space, hence claiming light as the known fastest object!

So light travels nearly 3,00,000 km in a second, 18000000 km in a minute, 1080000000 km in an hour, 25920000000 km in a day and 9467280000000 km in a year.

Light year is a unit of astronomical distance equivalent to the distance that light travels in one year.

But is 'light' the fastest?

No!

We believe that there exists something faster than light.

Farther it travels than what light can reach in a second, minute, day or year - MIND.

Mind; the most underrated traveler, which is capable of traveling back or sally forth making the term 'impossible' as just another word in dictionary. We fondly call the time travel of mind as 'Memories' or 'Imagination' depending on the direction of journey.

Let's usher in for a journey to the infinity. A journey to the edge of the observable universe, traversing through the multifarious discoveries beyond the visible stars and galaxies.

So, let's buckle up and dive into imagination with a speed of ONE LIGHT YEAR / Second, to traverse the known and unknown.

As we launch ourselves into the cosmic sphere, we will fly by the prominent objects discovered so far including stars, planets, galaxies, black holes, and like, learning the details of each.

We welcome, all you readers to join the journey with limitless imagination to know about the Universe.

Let's do the time travel.

Route Map

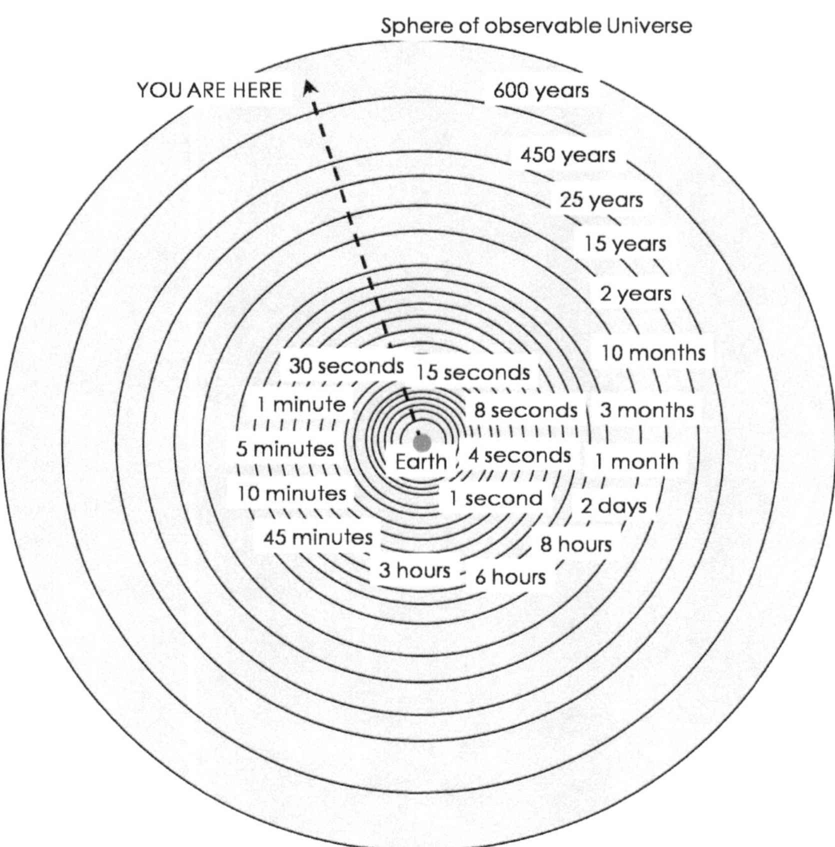

A 13.8 billion year old Universe with an estimated radius of 46.5 billion light years

No, it's not an Earth centric system. But we consider a celestial sphere and will travel radially outward, with each of the circles representing halts in the journey, detailed as chapters of this book.

One second

It took a blink of an eye to traverse the solar system.

Standing on the edge of the Oort Cloud, at the farthest reaches of the solar system, I behold a sight few have imagined seeing firsthand. Slightly less than a second ago, I was at the busy streets of Taverekere, leading to Nexus Mall, Koramangala, Bangalore, Karnataka, India, Planet Earth.

The solar system, seen from this distant vantage point, is a tiny, delicate oasis of light and motion set against the vast backdrop of interstellar space. From here, the Sun appears as a bright, but no longer overpowering, star, its golden glow diminished yet unmistakable in its brilliance. It is the central anchor of the solar system, around which everything orbits. The distant warmth of the Sun reaches even this far, a faint reminder of the nuclear furnace that fuels our cosmic neighborhood.

Surrounding the Sun, the planets trace their intricate paths. Closest to the Sun, Mercury is barely visible, a tiny, swift-moving dot. Venus shines more brightly, a beacon of pale light. Earth, our home, appears as a distinct blue dot, accompanied by its companion, the Moon, a smaller point of light. Mars, the Red Planet, glows with a subtle, rusty hue.

Further out, the gas giants dominate the scene. Jupiter, with its immense size, shines brightly, its many moons creating a miniature system of their own. Saturn, distinguished by its stunning rings, adds a majestic touch to the panorama. Uranus and Neptune, the ice giants, are faint, distant orbs tinged with blue-green light, their atmospheres rich with mysterious gases.

Beyond the planets, the Kuiper Belt spreads out, a vast ring of icy bodies and dwarf planets. Pluto, once considered the ninth planet, is a notable member, orbiting in this region with its own moons. As I gaze upon Pluto, I see its icy surface reflecting the dim sunlight, its largest moon Charon closely accompanying it in a mutual dance.

The Oort Cloud itself, where I stand, is a distant, spherical shell of icy bodies that envelops the solar system. Composed of countless comets and debris, it marks the boundary between the gravitational influence of the Sun and the vastness of interstellar space. These icy objects, frozen relics from the solar system's formation, lie in deep, cold slumber, waiting for some gravitational nudge to send them journeying toward the inner solar system.

The Oort Cloud extends up to a light-year from the Sun, its icy inhabitants loosely bound by the Sun's gravity. Together, the Kuiper Belt and the Oort Cloud form the outer frontier of our solar system. The Kuiper Belt, with its relatively flat, disk-like structure, is more densely populated and lies closer to the Sun, while the Oort Cloud, a vast spherical halo, marks the boundary of the Sun's gravitational influence. Both regions are filled with ancient ice and rock, holding clues to the early solar system and the processes that shaped it.

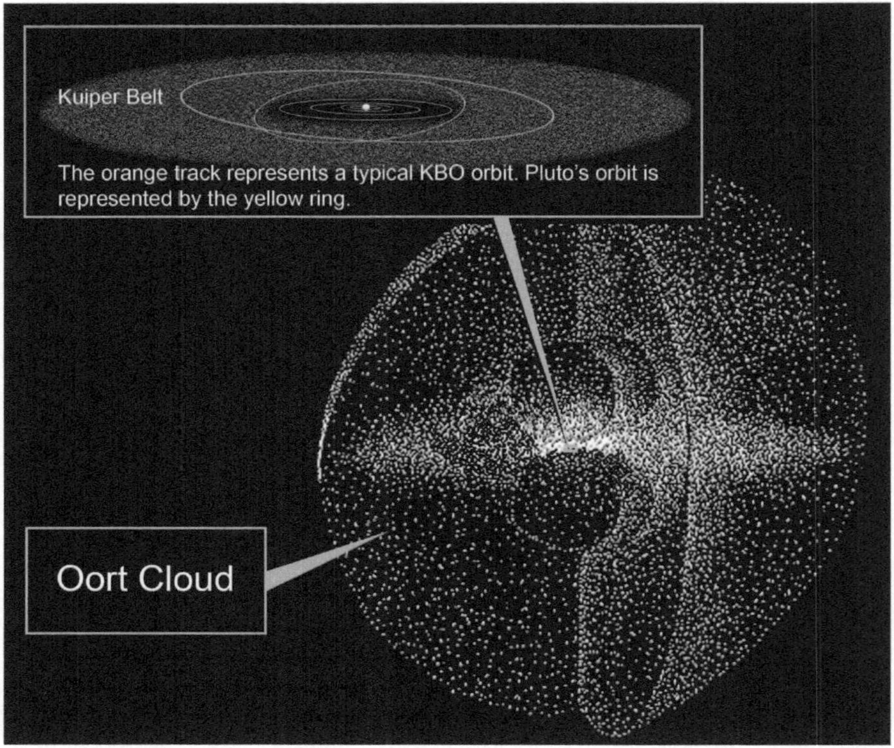

An illustration of the Kuiper Belt and Oort Cloud in relation to our solar system (courtesy: NASA)

As I turn my attention to the Kuiper Belt, a vast, donut-shaped region that extends beyond the orbit of Neptune. The sun is illuminating the icy denizens that populate Kuiper Belt which is teeming with small, icy bodies, remnants from the early solar system, known as Kuiper Belt Objects (KBO).

The Kuiper Belt is a dynamic region, where objects occasionally collide or are nudged by the gravitational influence of the giant planets, sending some inward toward the Sun or outward into the more distant Oort Cloud. The faint, diffuse light from the Sun casts long shadows on the surfaces of these icy bodies, creating an ethereal landscape of frozen relics.

From this vantage point, the solar system feels both immense and intimate. The vast distances between objects are staggering, yet the interconnectedness of the Sun, planets, and distant icy bodies forms a coherent, dynamic whole. The interplay of gravity, light, and motion creates a celestial dance that has been ongoing for billions of years.

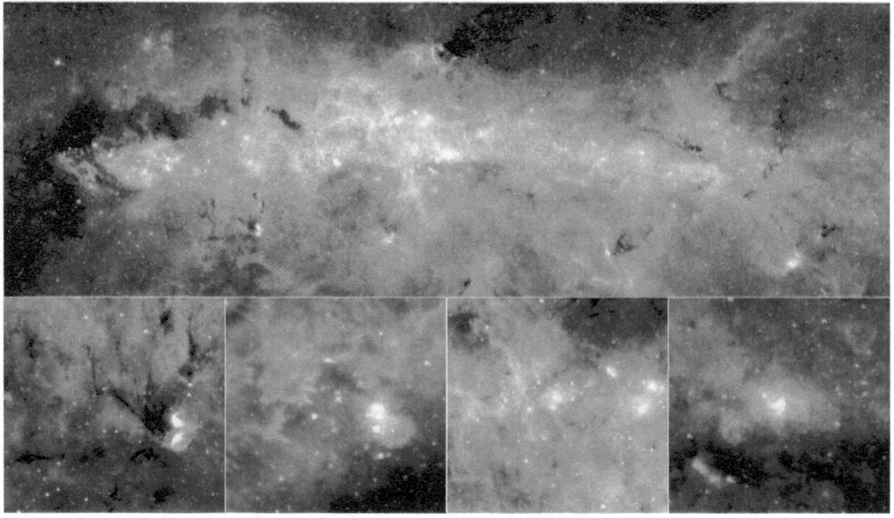

Dust in the center of the Milky Way Galaxy; Spitzer Space Telescope, IRAC ssc2006-02b (courtesy: NASA)

The Milky Way stretches across the sky, a dense band of stars and cosmic clouds, reminding me that our solar system is just one part of a much larger galaxy, itself one of billions in the universe. This perspective from the Oort Cloud offers a humbling view of our place in the cosmos, a fragile system of light and life set against the infinite darkness of space.

Standing here, I am filled with awe at the beauty and complexity of the solar system. It is a reminder of the wonders of the universe and the remarkable fact that, on a tiny blue dot within this vast expanse, life has found a way to thrive.

CHAPTER II

Four seconds

After 4 seconds of our journey, I reached a triple star system, the Alpha Centauri.

This is the closest star system at a distance of 4.2 light years from earth and brightest celestial object in the constellation Centaurus. This fascinating system comprise of Rigil Kentaurus (Alpha Centauri A), Toliman (Alpha Centauri B) and Proxima Centauri (Alpha Centauri C) which is gravitationally bound to Alpha Centauri A and B.

Alpha Centauri A and Alpha Centauri B (AB pair) are sun-like stars forming a binary system. Rigil is the fourth brightest star in the night sky with mass 1.1 times and 1.5 time luminous than that of Sun. This dazzling star is similar to the Sun with its spectral type G2 making it a yellow dwarf and surface temperature around 5790 K. While Toliman is cooler than Sun with its mass is 0.9 times the sun's mass, luminosity 0.5 times and surface temperature around 5260 K. This binary system orbits a common center of gravity (barycenter) once in every 80 years in an eccentric elliptical path with an average distance of 23.6 AU, similar to the distance between Sun and Uranus.

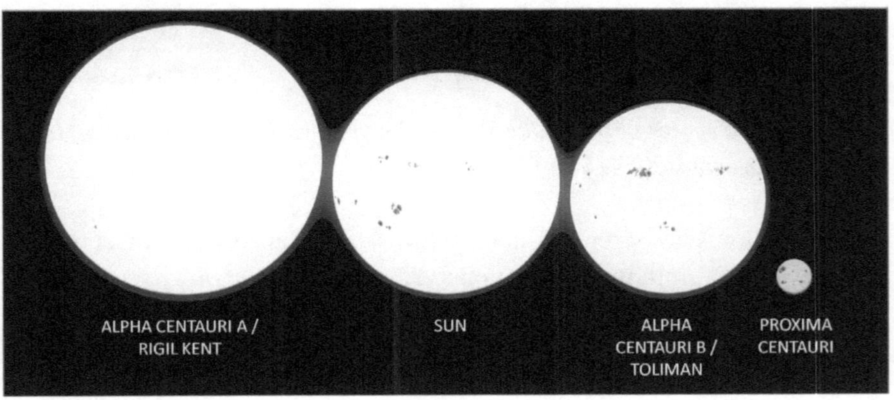

Alpha Centauri A and B are similar in size to the Sun, with Alpha Centauri A being slightly larger and B slightly smaller, while Proxima Centauri, the closest star to the Sun, is a much smaller red dwarf.

Proxima Centauri, the closest star from Earth next to Sun, is an active Red Dwarf which was discovered by Scottish astronomer Robert Thorburn Ayton Innes. This red dwarf is 4.2 light years from earth with mass nearly 12.5% of the sun. It is the dimmest star of the system with only 0.16% as luminous as sun. But at the same time, this small star produces enthralling flares generating X-ray emissions similar to that of the Sun.

On May 1, 2019, a flare 100 times brighter than the sun's largest flare was observed emerging from Proxima Centauri which lasted for 7 seconds. This record breaking flare was 1000 times brighter than any other flare from it. In 2016, proxima centauri's first superflare was noted, which was so radiant for observers to spot it even with naked eyes.

It is a main sequencer star having nuclear fusion at its core, turning hydrogen to helium gradually turning it into a White dwarf. However, the energy produced by it is at a lower rate than that in Sun.

Latest study confirms the existance of five Exo-planets in the Alpha Centauri system, three of which orbits Proxima Centauri and two orbiting Toliman. This includes Alpha Centauri Bb, which is 10 times closer than mercury to the Sun. The surface of this planet is enveloped by intense heat hot enough for it to molten lava with temperature of 1500 K. One year of this sizzling hot planet passes only in 3.2 Earth day. However Alpha Centauri Bc is learnt to be an terrestrial Earth-like planet with a 20-Earth day orbit.

Astronomers are more confident about the planets of Proxima centauri. Proxima centauri b lies in the habitable zone of proxima centauri and is considered as Super-Earth. This planet was discovered using Radial velocity method using the HARPS spectrograph on the ESO 3.6 m telescope in Chile. It has an orbital period of 11.2 Earth days and a semi major axis of 0.0485 AU. Its location is favourable for its surface for liquid water to exist. However the flares from proxima centauri might strip away its atmosphere creating conditions not suitable for life, if sufficiently strong magnetic field doesn't exist. Its potential habitability is also learnt to be affected since it is tidally locked with its one side perennially facing the star and other is constant darkness of the space.

Proxima centauri c is a mini-Neptune having thicker gaseous atmosphere. Its existance was confirmed in 2020 by the team led by Mario Damasso with the images from Hubble Space Telescope taken in 1995. It has an orbital period of 5.2 Earth years with distance from the star around 1.5 AU making it more likely to be colder than Earth. As per latest findings Proxima centauri c remains as a potential candidate and additional observations are needed to confirm its characteristics.

Another candidate of Poxima centauri is Proxima centauri d which was detected in 2022 again with radial velocity method using ESPRESSO instrument on Very Large Telescope (VLT). It is one of the lightest exoplanet found by astronomers and is having 25% of Earth's mass and is closer to the star by only 0.0228 AU. It has an orbital period of 5.15 Earth days and is likely to be rocky having extreme temperatures and strong stellar radiations creating bleak environment for life.

Hopefully, in future, an interstellar journey may happen which can give us a taste of these planets those can be the next home to humanity.

CHAPTER III

Eight seconds

While on Earth, looking up at the night sky, like any of you, my eyes were also irresistibly drawn to the brilliant sparkle of Sirius, the brightest star in the firmament.

Travelling 8.6 light years from our planet, I have arrived at the brightest star in the night sky which dominate, as a beacon of clarity and constancy.

Positioned in the constellation Canis Major, Sirius dazzles with a luminosity that outshines all others, earning its rightful title as the "Dog Star." (since it is located in the constellation Canis Major, also known as the "Great Dog"). With an apparent magnitude of -1.46, Sirius is the brightest star in the night sky, shining nearly twice as brightly as the second-brightest star, Canopus.

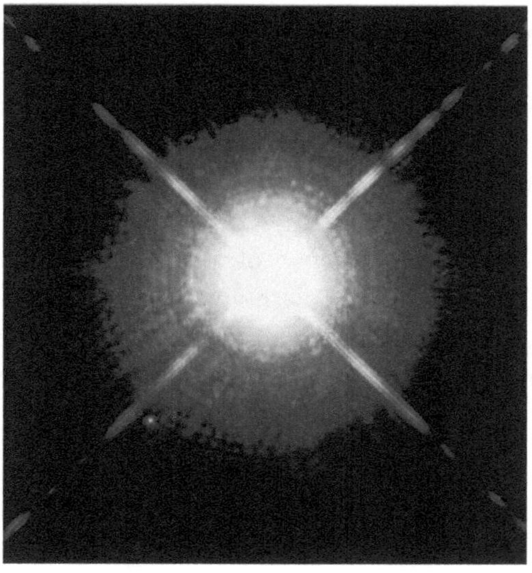

Sirius A and B (lower left) photographed by the Hubble Space Telescope (courtesy: ESA)

Sirius radiates a stunning bluish-white light, casting a serene glow that pierces the darkness. Its intense brightness is due not only to its intrinsic luminosity but also to its relative proximity to Earth.

All of us have sung the nursery rhyme 'Twinkle, twinkle little star' atleast once watching the glimmering sirius. Let's thank Jane Taylor for this amazing poem and its time to re-write this for Sirius now.

"Twinkle, twinkle, Sirius bright,
Gleaming in the dark of night.
Up above, you shine so near,
Guiding us with light so clear.
Twinkle, twinkle, Sirius bright,
Beacon in the sky's twilight".

As I continue to wonder, memories of it is twinkling with remarkable intensity flashed in my mind.

I remember, *Arun* explaining about this scintillation 'as the result of its light passing through the Earth's turbulent atmosphere, causing the star to flicker and shimmer in a captivating dance'.

The effect is mesmerizing, as if Sirius is a living jewel, pulsing with the energy of the cosmos.

In the stillness of the night, the mythological and historical significance of Sirius comes to mind. Known to ancient civilizations, Sirius was revered and studied by cultures around the world. To the Egyptians, it heralded the annual flooding of the Nile, a vital event for their agriculture. The Greeks associated it with the dog of Orion, the hunter, cementing its place in the rich tapestry of human storytelling.

As I stand beneath the expanse of the universe, with Sirius shining brilliantly before me, I am filled with a sense of wonder and connection. This star, blazing so brightly in the night, is a reminder of the vastness of space and the timeless beauty of celestial bodies.

CHAPTER IV

Fifteen seconds

At about 11 seconds of my journey, I found a temperate exoplanet Ross 128b, orbiting the red dwarf Ross 128 with potential habitability. The first thing which came to my mind looking at Ross 128 b, is the distance to travel for Earthlings to land and settle there. It works out to be 104137.22 billion kilometres (11 light years), which demands faster Space transportation systems compared to those existing. Located in the constellation Virgo, Ross 128 b orbits within its star's habitable zone, where liquid water could exist. The planet itself appears as a rocky world, possibly similar in size and composition to Earth.

One light year away from Ross 128b, two more planets GJ 1061 d and GJ 1061 c orbiting the red dwarf GJ 1061 can be found. As I reach near, GJ 1061 d is seen to my left and GJ 1061 c to the right in their respective orbits. GJ 1061 d lies in the habitable zone of its star, with rocky surface with conditions that could support liquid water. The faint, cool light of GJ 1061 highlights the serene and potentially life-sustaining environment, with a quiet, steady illumination. Meanwhile, GJ 1061 c is slightly in a smaller orbit. The surface feels more intense with its star's light, indicating a warmer climate. The potential for habitability remains intriguing, as this rocky exoplanet could have conditions suitable for sustaining liquid water under certain atmospheric conditions.

Another orbiting planet caught my attention as I was calculating the possibilities of alien life. Luyten b, another potentially habitable world with a temperate environment, is orbiting the red dwarf Luyten's Star (GJ 273) in the Canis Minor constellation. The planet orbits within the habitable zone, where the right atmospheric conditions could allow liquid water to exist.

At 12.5 light-years away from Earth in the Aries, subsists another bi-planetary system orbiting the ultra-cool red dwarf Teegarden's Star - the planets Teegarden's Star b & c qualifies for consideration of candidacy for habitability. Teegarden's Star b resides in the habitable zone, and its proximity to its star suggests a warm, potentially life-sustaining environment. Teegarden's Star c is slightly farther out than Teegarden's Star b and this planet might be cooler but still lies within the habitable zone. The subdued, red light from Teegarden's Star envelops the planet, offering a view of a potentially rocky surface with conditions that might support liquid water, depending on its atmosphere.

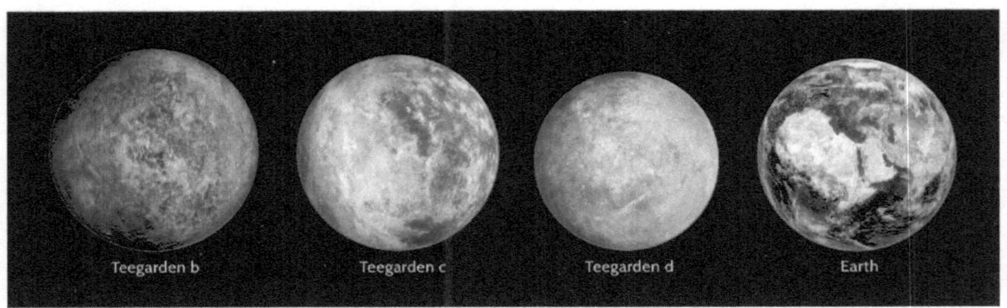

Comparing potentially habitable planets - Teegarden's planets & Earth

Possibly some alien life form might have evolved in these habitable zones, flourished and who knows when or whether perished.

Aren't we defining habitability based on our requirements to exist, like water, oxygen etc?

Pondering deep into such weirdly beautiful concepts, another rocky planet appeared slightly far off.

Wolf 1061c, a rocky landscape potentially similar to that of Earth, seems tranquil and conducive to life orbits the red dwarf Wolf 1061, about 14 light-years away in Ophiuchus, one of the 48 constellations listed by the 2nd-century astronomer Ptolemy. Standing here, the planet appears within its star's habitable zone, suggesting it could support liquid water.

Two other planets GJ 1002 b and GJ 1002 c orbits the red dwarf GJ 1002 at nearly 16 light-years away from Earth, both potentially habitable with possible liquid water in rocky surface.

Each of these exoplanets presents a unique and fascinating environment, offering tantalizing possibilities for habitability and the existence of life beyond our solar system.

CHAPTER V

Thirty seconds

Moving further into another 15 seconds, I enter into an arena of many exoplanets around red dwarfs star named Gliese lying in various constellations. It seems I've entered a huge atomic nucleus where electrons around are illuminated as stars and their planets orbiting.

At the centre of a mini Universe.

One of such red dwarf is Gliese 229 which is at about 18.8 light years in the constellation Lepus. Gliese 229 (Gl 229) exists as a binary system having a red dwarf and the first observed brown dwarf. Its weight is estimated to be nearly half of Sun and size nearly 69% of Sun.

Multiple exoplanets were discovered around this star, of which Gliese 229 Ac, a super-Neptune mass planet, is prominent. It orbits relatively close to its host star, likely within a region that influences its climate and atmospheric conditions significantly. The red dwarf star, being cooler and dimmer than our Sun, meaning the planet receives a lower amount of stellar radiation, potentially affecting its surface temperature and habitability. While specific details about the planet's atmosphere, composition, and potential for supporting life are still under investigation, its proximity to Earth makes it a valuable target for future observational campaigns and research efforts aimed at uncovering the mysteries of exoplanetary environments.

Gliese 625 b, another exoplanet located approximately 21 light-years away from Earth in the constellation Draco orbits another red dwarf star Gliese 625. This is classified as a super-Earth due to its size and mass. Observations and studies of Gliese 625 b continue to provide valuable insights into the nature of super-Earths and the potential for life beyond our solar system.

At approximately 23.62 light-years away in the constellation Scorpius lies Gliese 667 Cc orbiting within the habitable zone of the red dwarf star Gliese 667 C, which is part of a triple-star system. As a super-Earth, Gliese 667 Cc has a mass at least 4.5 times that of Earth, suggesting it may have a rocky composition receiving about 90% of the light that Earth gets from the Sun, much of which is in the infrared spectrum due to its host star's characteristics. Gliese 667 Cc's location in a triple-star system adds to its uniqueness, with the gravitational interactions of its neighboring stars potentially influencing its orbit and climate. The planet's discovery has excited astronomers and astrobiologists alike, making it a prime target for further study in the quest to find potentially habitable worlds beyond our solar system.

Similarly, Gliese 514 b at 24.85 light-years in the Virgo constellation, Gliese 433 d and Gliese 357 d at nearly 30 light-years in the Hydra constellation, Gliese 180 c & d at 39 light-years in the Eridanus constellation are potential habitable Earth-like planets discovered in the beginning of 21st century.

A shining gem amidst these planetary systems blinded me while I was panning around.

NASA's Spitzer Space Telescope was able to detect the heat radiation from the cloud of dust around Vega and found that the debris disc is much larger than previously thought (courtesy: NASA)

It's Vega, one of the brightest stars in Earth's night sky at about 25 light-years from Earth in the constellation Lyra. This A-type main-sequence star shines with a brilliant blue-white hue and has an apparent magnitude of 0.03, making it the fifth brightest star visible from Earth. For us Earthlings, It is also known as Alpha Lyrae, a prominent feature in the night sky, particularly during the summer months in the Northern Hemisphere. It has been extensively studied due to its relatively simple spectrum and its role as a standard calibration star for brightness measurements. A rotational speed of approximately 236 km/s at its equator is a unique feature of Vega and the rapid rotation causes the star to have an oblate shape, with a noticeable bulge around its equator.

I was wondering about the debris that surrounds Vega as a disc of dust similar to Kuiper Belt in our solar system, which may be an indication of planet-forming processes.

Vega was the first star other than the Sun to be photographed and to have its spectrum recorded. It also served as the pole star around 12,000 BC and will do so again in the future due to the precession of the Earth's axis.

As I look above me, in the constellation Cygnus, I could see an intriguing exoplanet named as Wolf 1069 b. It orbits the red dwarf star Wolf 1069, which is smaller and cooler than our Sun. Observations and studies of Wolf 1069 b aim to uncover more about its atmosphere, climate, and potential for habitability, making it a significant target in the search for extraterrestrial life.

Slightly away from Cygnus, lies the Volans constellation where L 98-59 planetary system exists that orbits a bright, relatively cool M-dwarf star. Discovered using the Transiting Exoplanet Survey Satellite (TESS), L 98-59 f is notable for being one of the planets in a compact system with at least five known exoplanets with possibility of liquid water. The star's relatively close proximity to Earth makes it an excellent target for follow-up observations with more powerful telescopes, such as the James Webb Space Telescope (JWST).

I felt some kind of pride remembering JWST at the L2 (Legrangian point-2) working as the eye of human race kept open towards the history of the universe.

The discovery of L 98-59 f and its neighboring planets contributes significantly to our understanding of planetary systems around M-dwarf stars, which are the most common type of stars in our galaxy.

Another bright star Arcturus also known as Alpha Boötis in the constellation Boötes and one of the most luminous stars visible from Earth stood distinct with its orange-red hue, which is a result of its cooler surface temperature compared to stars like our Sun. With a diameter about 25 times greater than that of the Sun and luminosity roughly 170 times that of the Sun, Arcturus is a prominent feature in the night sky of Earth. This star is in the later stages of its life cycle, having exhausted the hydrogen in its core and expanded as it burns helium.

Arcturus has historical significance and has been used in various cultures for navigation and timekeeping. It also played a role in the 1933 Chicago World's Fair, where its light, having travelled for 40 years, was used to open the fair.

Adjacent to Boötes lies the constellation Serpens, which houses a red dwarf star Ross 508 known for its relatively low luminosity and cool temperature compared to our Sun. An intriguing exoplanet Ross 508 b approximately at 36.9 light-years away from Earth is classified as a super-Earth.

As I walk past these glowing red dwarfs to brilliant blue giants, the cosmic landscape around me is filled with wonders waiting to be explored deeper.

CHAPTER VI

One minute

In about 40 s duration of the journey I encountered the TRAPPIST-1 system, which is an extraordinary exoplanetary system located about 40 light-years away in the constellation Aquarius.

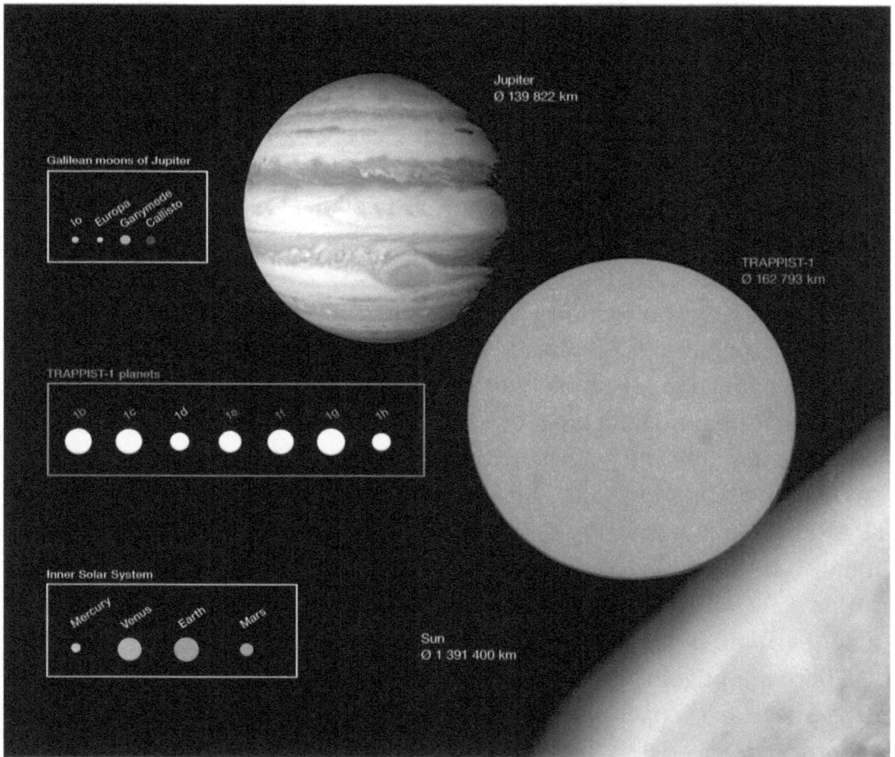

Size comparisson between Trappist-1 system, Galilean moons of Jupiter and the inner solar system

It's another solar system with one planet less than what we have.

Named after the Transiting Planets and Planetesimals Small Telescope (TRAPPIST) in Chile, which first discovered the system, this is particularly notable because it contains seven Earth-sized planets, three of which reside in the star's habitable zone, where conditions might be right for liquid water to exist.

TRAPPIST-1 is an ultra-cool red dwarf star, much smaller and cooler than our Sun. With only about 9% of the Sun's mass and roughly 12% of its radius, it emits only a fraction of the sunlight, resulting in a dim red glow.

he curious kid in me woke up in the quest of search for extra terrestrial intelligence, rather habitable worlds. Let's land on each of these planets and understand the possibilities.

Discovered in 2017, TRAPPIST-1b is the innermost planet in the planetary system this planet and stands out for its proximity to its host star, offering a unique window into the dynamics of tightly-packed planetary systems. The distance to the star is about 0.011 AU, which is roughly 1% of the distance between Earth and the Sun. With a radius approximately 1.12 times that of Earth, it completes an orbit around its star in just 1.5 Earth days, making its 'year' incredibly short. The planet's density is similar to or slightly higher than Earth's, suggesting a rocky composition and its mass is roughly 1.02 times Earth's mass.

Due to its close proximity to TRAPPIST-1, TRAPPIST-1b experiences extreme temperatures, estimated to be around 400-500 K (127-227°C or 260-440°F), making it unlikely to host liquid water on its surface. Due to the gravitational tidal locking, one side always faces the star, resulting in a scorching day side and a perpetually dark night side.

Given its proximity to the host star and the resulting high temperatures, TRAPPIST-1b is not considered to be within the habitable zone where liquid water could exist on the surface. However, studying its atmosphere can provide valuable insights into atmospheric composition and dynamics under extreme stellar radiation.

There are ongoing efforts to characterize the atmosphere of the planet using space telescopes like the Hubble Space Telescope and the JWST. Scientists aim to detect the presence of gases such as hydrogen, helium, water vapor, and more, which can help understand the planet's formation and evolution.

Standing on the surface of TRAPPIST-1b, we can see the TRAPPIST-1 star dominating the sky, appearing much larger than our Sun does from Earth due to the planet's close orbit.

Moving on to the second planet TRAPPIST-1c, this is about 1.10 times in radius that of Earth, we find a rocky planetary surface with a possibly dense iron core. This orbits the star at a distance of about 0.0158 AU , which is about 1.6% of the distance between Earth and the Sun. TRAPPIST-1c completes an orbit around its star in approximately 2.42 Earth days. Even though the mass is approximately 1.16 times Earth's mass, it has got similar density as of Earth.

TRAPPIST-1c receives about 2.1 times the stellar flux that Earth does, leading to surface temperatures estimated to be around 334 K (61°C or 142°F), which might be too hot for liquid water to exist on the surface without a thick atmosphere to distribute the heat. Similar to the first planet, here also one side always faces the star, due to tidal locking.

Scientists look for gases such as water vapor, carbon dioxide, and methane, which could provide clues about the planet's climate and potential for habitability.

Landing on the third planet, with anticipation of another Earth, in TRAPPIST-1d, we can experience the presence of an atmosphere with possible liquid water.

This planet completes an orbit around its star in about 4.05 Earth days, with its orbital distance at approximately 0.022 AU, which is about 2.2% of the distance between Earth and the Sun. It has got radius 0.78 times that of Earth, while mass is roughly 0.39 times Earth's mass and density lower compared to that of Earth.

TRAPPIST-1d receives about 4.3% of the sunlight Earth does, which places its equilibrium temperature in a range that could allow for liquid water under the right atmospheric conditions. Estimated surface temperatures are around 282 K (9°C or 48°F), assuming a moderate greenhouse effect. Only risk towards chances of life is the possible tidal locking which could create extreme temperature differences between the day side and the night side.

Its location within the habitable zone of its star, combined with its Earth-like size and potential atmospheric conditions, makes it a key target for ongoing and future observations aimed at uncovering the mysteries of distant, potentially life-supporting worlds.

TRAPPIST-1e is the fourth planet from the star in the system, which completes an orbit around its star in about 6.1 Earth days. It orbits at a distance of approximately 0.029 AU. The radius of this planet is comparable to that of Earth (0.92 times Earth's radius), while mass is nearly 0.77 times Earth's mass. It has got density similar to or slightly higher than Earth's, suggesting a rocky composition with a significant iron core.

This planet receives about 60% of the sunlight Earth does, which places it comfortably within the habitable zone. The estimated equilibrium temperature is around 251 K (-22°C or -8°F), which could allow for liquid water on its surface under the right atmospheric conditions. Even though constrain of tidal locking exists; TRAPPIST-1e is one of the promising candidates for habitability within the system due to its location in the habitable zone and Earth-like characteristics.

If the atmosphere is dense enough, it can distribute heat effectively across the planet, potentially creating a more uniform climate that could support liquid water and, possibly, life. TRAPPIST-1e stands out as one of the most compelling exoplanets for the search for life beyond our solar system.

Fifth planet TRAPPIST-1f completes an orbit around its star in about 9.2 Earth days. The orbit distance is approximately 0.037 AU, which is about 3.7% of the distance between Earth and the Sun. It is 1.04 times that of Earth in size and has 0.68 times Earth's mass. With density lower than that of Earth, TRAPPIST-1f may have a significant amount of water or a thick atmosphere.

Like its sibling planets, TRAPPIST-1f is likely tidally locked and it receives about 38% of the sunlight Earth does, placing it in the outer edge of the habitable zone. The estimated equilibrium temperature is around 219 K (-54°C or -65°F), which could allow for liquid water under specific atmospheric conditions.

TRAPPIST-1g, the sixth planet in the system completes an orbit around its star in about 12.4 Earth days, at an orbit distance of approximately 0.045 AU, which is about 4.5% of the distance between Earth and the Sun. Radius of this planet is approximately 1.15 times that of Earth, mass is roughly 1.34 times that of Earth with lower density than Earth composition.

Likely tidally locked, TRAPPIST-1g receives about 26% of the sunlight Earth does, placing it within the habitable zone where liquid water might exist if the atmospheric conditions are right. The estimated equilibrium temperature is around 198 K (-75°C or -103°F), but with a thick atmosphere, this temperature could be higher.

The last and farthest planet TRAPPIST-1h is revolving around the star at a distance of approximately 0.063 AU, which is about 6.3% of the distance between Earth and the Sun. It completes an orbit around its star in about 18.8 Earth days. With an approximate radius of 0.77 times that of Earth and a mass of around 0.33 times Earth's mass, TRAPPIST-1h is considered to have a thick, icy crust.

This planet receives about 13% of the sunlight Earth does, placing it beyond the traditional habitable zone. The estimated equilibrium temperature is around 173 K (-100°C or -148°F), indicating a very cold environment where water, if present, would likely be frozen.

TRAPPIST-1h, in comparison with its warmer siblings, helps to illustrate the diversity of planetary environments within the same system. While TRAPPIST-1h is less likely to host life as we know it due to its cold environment and tidal locking, it remains a fascinating target for astronomical research.

As I am leaving the system after expedition in search of habitable planets, I realize that all the seven planets are all closer to their star than Mercury is to our Sun. Their tight orbits and similar sizes to Earth make them unique among exoplanetary systems, even though tidal locking prevents them from changing day and night.

With a hope that someday the scientific community come up with discoveries of life possibility in TRAPPIST-1 system, I am flying by the star and its planets, bidding adieu, in search of newer horizons. As I travel past a a K-type main-sequence star named HD 40307, at approximately 45 light-years away in the constellation Pictor star, I noticed an exoplanet named as HD 40307 g. This, exoplanet, I felt as noteworthy because it resides in the star's habitable zone, where conditions might allow for the presence of liquid water, a key ingredient for life as we know it.

HD 40307 g in an orbit which is approximately 0.6 AU completes a resolution around its star in about 197.8 Earth days. It has an estimated radius of about 1.9 times that of Earth and approximate mass of 7.1 times Earth's mass.

Given its proximity to its star, HD 40307 g might be tidally locked similar to the Trappist-1 planets. This planet seems to be receiving about 66% of the sunlight Earth does, placing it within the habitable zone. The equilibrium temperature is estimated to be around 247 K (-26°C or -15°F). With a suitable atmosphere, this temperature could be higher, allowing for liquid water.

Similarly few more planets are found in the vicinity including LHS 1140 b which is 7 times heavier than Earth, Gliese 163 c which is twice the size of Earth and the mysterious GJ 3293 d. The telescopes which tell us the stories of past and searches possibilities of future are keenly behind such planetary systems in search of a new home for humanity.

CHAPTER VII

Five minutes

Imagine standing in the vastness of space, floating in front of a blue Earth-like planet.

An exoplanet K2-18b also known as EPIC 201912552, with liquid ocean on the surface, at about 124 light-years away from Earth in the Leo constellation is promising in the quest towards potential habitable worlds. It's a sub-Neptune about 2.6 times radius of Earth, with 33 day orbit within the star's habitable zone. What sets K2-18b apart is its potential to host liquid water, a key ingredient for life as we know it. Scientists have detected water vapour in the atmosphere of K2-18b, making it the first exoplanet outside our solar system where water vapour has been found. This discovery has sparked excitement and speculation about the possibility of habitability on this distant world. In 2019, JWST detected Carbon-dioxide and Methane in the atmosphere of the planet. It is likely tidally locked to the star which limits the habitable zone to the delineating lines of day and night.

With a stronger gravitational pull than Earth, I feel myself heavier while standing on this blue planet, and the sky appears different, due to the composition of its atmosphere. There are clouds drifting overhead, and there's a thick haze obscuring view of the stars.

In two minutes of our journey, I have reached the Dorado constellation where the planet TOI-700 d with blend of blue, with green, and brown, indicating the presence of water bodies, landmasses, and possibly vegetation.

It is a fascinating exoplanet orbiting the red dwarf star TOI-700, located about 101.5 light-years away in the constellation Dorado. This exoplanet has captured the imagination of scientists and space enthusiasts alike due to its Earth-like qualities and its position within the habitable zone of its star.

As I was gazing upon TOI-700 d, I see a planet that resembles a larger, slightly darker version of Earth. Wisps of white clouds swirl in the atmosphere, hinting at dynamic weather patterns. The terminator line, where day meets night, casts a shadow that slowly creeps across the planet's surface, creating a stunning interplay of light and shadow.

TOI-700 d orbits its red dwarf star at a distance that places it within the habitable zone, where conditions might allow for liquid water to exist.

The star TOI-700 is much cooler and redder than our Sun, casting a warm, reddish glow on the planet. Despite the star's lower luminosity, its close proximity to the planet ensures that it receives enough energy to potentially support life.

TOI-700 d is slightly larger than Earth, with a radius about 1.14 times that of our home planet. Its mass is also slightly higher, suggesting a solid, rocky composition. This super-Earth likely has a robust atmosphere, contributing to its ability to sustain temperate conditions on its surface.

Standing in front of this planet, I am imagining a world with a variety of landscapes: expansive oceans, towering mountain ranges, and vast plains. The temperature on the surface would be temperate, thanks to its favorable position in the habitable zone. Depending on the exact composition of its atmosphere, the climate could range from warm and tropical to cool and temperate.

The atmosphere of TOI-700 d is a subject of great interest. It could be rich in nitrogen, oxygen, and possibly other gases such as carbon dioxide and water vapor, creating conditions suitable for life as we know it. The presence of clouds and weather systems suggests an active atmosphere that can distribute heat evenly across the planet, potentially preventing extreme temperature variations between the day and night sides if the planet is tidally locked.

Its Earth-like size, favorable position within the habitable zone, and the potential for a rich atmosphere make it a prime target for future observational missions. Its striking appearance, temperate climate, and potential for habitability make it a beacon of hope in the ongoing quest to find life beyond our own planet.

In the constellation Eridanus, in the same celestial sphere of TOI-700 d lies the P 890-9 c, an intriguing exoplanet orbiting the red dwarf star LP 890-9, also known as SPECULOOS-2 presents a dark, rocky world. Its surface might be punctuated by vast stretches of land, potentially dotted with large water bodies or ice-covered regions. The planet's surface could be a mix of gray and brown hues, with patches of green indicating possible vegetation if life-supporting conditions exist. Tufts of clouds might be seen moving across the atmosphere, suggesting active weather patterns.

LP 890-9 c orbits its star at a distance that places it within the habitable zone, where conditions might allow for liquid water to exist. Despite the red dwarf star LP 890-9 having lower luminosity, the planet is close enough to receive sufficient warmth, potentially creating a temperate environment.

LP 890-9 c is a super-Earth, larger than our planet but smaller than Neptune, with a radius approximately 1.37 times that of Earth. Its mass, inferred from its size, suggests a rocky composition, similar to Earth but with a potentially thicker atmosphere that could include a mix of nitrogen, oxygen, and other gases.

The atmosphere of LP 890-9 c could be rich in gases necessary for life, such as nitrogen, oxygen, carbon dioxide, and water vapor.

At approximately 285 light-years away from Earth, in Eridanus constellation itself, another exoplanet TOI-715 b orbits the star TOI-715, a K-type main-sequence star slightly smaller and cooler than our Sun.

TOI-715 b completes its orbit around its host star in approximately 12.6 Earth days with an orbital distance of about 0.1 AU, which is only 10% of the distance between Earth and the Sun. This proximity places it very close to its star, likely resulting in a very hot environment. The planet has a radius approximately 2.1 times that of Earth, categorizing it as a mini-Neptune, likely having a thick atmosphere composed primarily of hydrogen and helium, with possible traces of water vapour, methane, and other gases.

As I proceed to the next planet K2-288Bb in the Taurus constellation, I see the sky above is tinged with a constant twilight, rugged landscape possibly featuring rocky terrains and expansive plains, with potential signs of water in the form of rivers or lakes if the atmosphere and temperature allow. The planet's gravity, slightly stronger than Earth's due to its larger mass, creates a sense of solid grounding beneath my feet.

Looking up, the binary stars' complex interplay creates unique visual phenomena, with the larger red star dominating the sky while the smaller one appears as a bright, distant companion. The potential for life, the geological features, and the atmospheric dynamics of K2-288Bb make it a world rich with possibilities and a prime focus for future exploration and study in the quest to understand the cosmos and our place within it.

Located approximately 226 light-years, K2-288Bb orbits at a distance of approximately 0.164 AU. The K2-288 system is a binary star system, consisting of two dim M-type (red dwarf) stars. The primary star appears much larger and redder in the sky compared to the Sun from Earth, casting a gentle, reddish hue across the landscape. The secondary star, though smaller and less bright, contributes to the complex dance of light and shadows on the planet's surface.

300 light-years away in the constellation Cygnus lies Kepler-1649c, often hailed as one of the most Earth-like exoplanets discovered in terms of size

and temperature, and its beauty and technical features, is nothing short of awe-inspiring.

Before me, the red dwarf star Kepler-1649 glows with a soft, crimson light. It appears larger and redder than our Sun due to the proximity of Kepler-1649c to its host star. The star's gentle, red illumination bathes the planet in a perpetual twilight, creating a surreal, almost ethereal atmosphere.

Kepler-1649c, slightly larger than Earth with about 1.06 times Earth's radius, presents a familiar yet alien landscape. From here, the planet's surface shows varying shades of blue, green, and brown, suggesting the presence of water bodies, landmasses, and possibly vegetation.

A thin veil of clouds can be seen, creating intricate patterns in the planet's atmosphere. The clouds catch the red light of the star, casting a rosy hue across the sky and creating breathtaking sunrises and sunsets.

It completes an orbit around its star in just about 19.5 Earth days, a rapid cycle that means seasons, if they exist, would change quickly compared to Earth. The planet orbits at a distance of about 0.082 AU, placing it in the habitable zone of its star where conditions could allow for liquid water.

As I complete five minutes of my expedition, I reach directly in front of the brilliant star Canopus, also known as Alpha Carinae, the second brightest star in the night sky after Sirius. Located about 310 light-years away in the constellation Carina, Canopus is a dazzling and awe-inspiring sight.

Canopus, the second-brightest star in the night sky, shines with a brilliant, white-yellow hue (courtesy: NASA)

I'm awe-struck by its sheer luminosity with a brilliant, white-yellow light, much brighter and more intense than any star visible from Earth. Its brightness is due to its intrinsic luminosity rather than proximity, making it one of the most luminous stars in our galaxy. Canopus is about 10,000 times more luminous than the Sun.

It is thus a bright giant or supergiant star, significantly larger and more massive than the Sun with diameter approximately 71 times that of the Sun and mass nearly 8 to 9 times the mass of the Sun.

The colour of the star is indicative of its spectral type, A9. This signifies that Canopus has a surface temperature of around 7,500 K (7,230°C or 13,040°F), much hotter than the Sun's surface.

In the space around Canopus, the star's intense light casts a glow on nearby cosmic dust and gas. The star's radiation pressure is so powerful that it shapes the surrounding interstellar medium, creating regions of illuminated gas and dark voids where the star's light cannot penetrate.

Canopus has exhausted the hydrogen in its core and is now fusing heavier elements. This stage of life means it has expanded significantly from its original size. Being a landmark in the sky, historically, Canopus has been used for navigation by sailors in the southern hemisphere.

CHAPTER VIII

Ten minutes

We all have wondered at a single, radiant star that seems to hold a special place amidst the celestial tapestry while gazing up at the night sky, during childhood days. It is Polaris, also known as Alpha Ursae Minoris, the brightest luminary in the constellation Ursa Minor, the Little Bear.

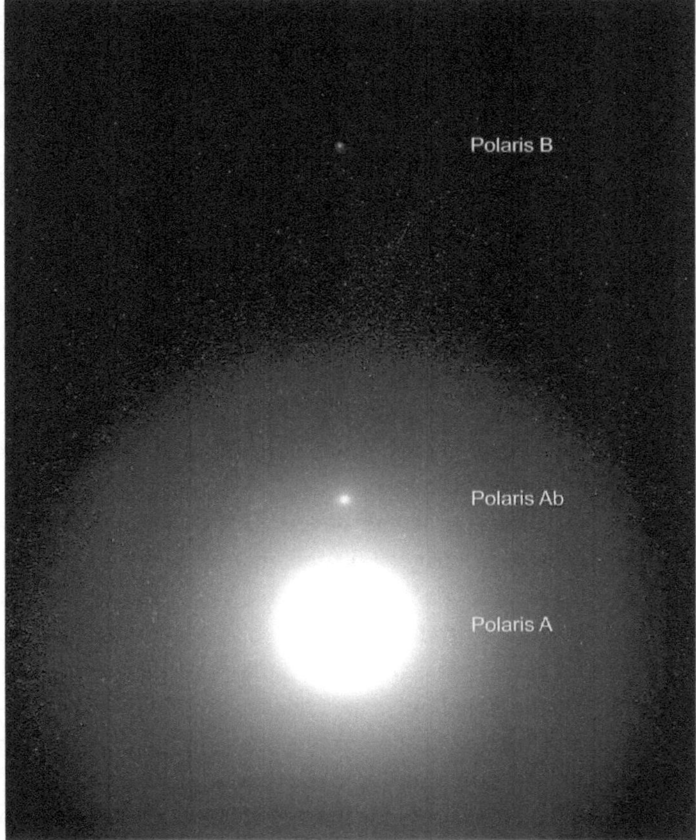

By stretching the capabilities of NASA's Hubble Space Telescope to the limit, astronomers photographed the close companion to Polaris, known also as the North Star, for the first time (courtesy: NASA)

Nearly ten minutes into the journey, we witness the star which we used to wonder about from planet Earth.

Polaris gleams with a steady, pale-white brilliance, standing out prominently against the backdrop of surrounding stars. Its luminosity, which fluctuates ever so slightly, grants it the status of being the North Star, a guiding light for navigators and dreamers alike. With a visual magnitude hovering around 1.97, Polaris ranks as one of the brightest stars visible to the naked eye. Ancient mariners relied on its unwavering position in the sky to guide their voyages across uncharted seas, while countless civilizations revered it as a symbol of stability and guidance in the ever-changing cosmos. Serving as a celestial compass needle, positioned less than a degree away from the north celestial pole, this star holds a privileged position in the sky, almost motionless as the Earth spins on its axis. Its proximity to the celestial pole makes it an invaluable reference point for travelers navigating across the globe and for astronomers charting the heavens.

While Polaris appears as a single point of light to the naked eye, it harbors a hidden secret which I realize standing gazing at it. Polaris is a binary star system, consisting of a primary star, Polaris A, and a smaller companion, Polaris B, orbiting each other in a celestial dance. Polaris A shines with the majority of the system's light, while Polaris B, a fainter and cooler companion, orbits at a distance.

Nearly at the same radial distance in celestial sphere, I have found myself in the presence of the Pleiades, one of the most famous and easily recognizable star clusters in the heavens.

The Pleiades, also known as the Seven Sisters, form a stunning sight against the dark canvas of space. Located in the constellation of Taurus, these stars have captivated the imaginations of astronomers, poets, and storytellers for millennia. At the heart of the Pleiades cluster lies a tight-knit group of hot, young stars, born from the same vast cloud of gas and dust that once roamed the cosmic landscape. These stars, known as B-type main sequence stars, burn with a brilliant blue-white light, casting a luminous glow that illuminates the surrounding darkness.

As I stand and gaze upon the Pleiades, I noticed the cluster appearing to be dominated by a handful of bright stars, often likened to a miniature version of the Big Dipper. These stars are the Seven Sisters of Greek mythology: Maia, Electra, Taygete, Alcyone, Celaeno, Sterope, and Merope. According to legend, these sisters were transformed into stars by the gods to escape the pursuit of Orion the Hunter.

But the Pleiades is not merely a cluster of stars; it is also a stellar nursery, giving birth to new generations of stars. Scattered throughout the cluster are countless fainter stars and protostars, each one a testament to the ongoing process of stellar birth and evolution.

Reaching 550 light years from Earth, I witness one of the fiery radiant stars in the Scorpius constellation. Antares, also known as Alpha Scorpii, is a luminous red supergiant with a diameter over 700 times that of our Sun, making it one of the largest known stars in the Milky Way galaxy.

Despite its grandeur, Antares burns with a tumultuous energy, its surface roiling and convulsing in a maelstrom of nuclear fusion. This turbulent activity gives rise to powerful stellar winds that cascade outward, sculpting the surrounding space and shaping the destiny of nearby celestial bodies.

Antares is classified as a variable star, meaning its brightness fluctuates over time. These variations are caused by pulsations in its outer layers. The name "Antares" is derived from the Ancient Greek word Ἀντάρης, meaning "opposing Ares" (the Greek god of war, equivalent to the Roman god Mars). It is thought to represent the heart of the scorpion in the constellation Scorpius.

Another distant exoplanet in the vicinity known as Kepler-22b, is a mesmerizing world, situated over 600 light-years away in the constellation of Cygnus.

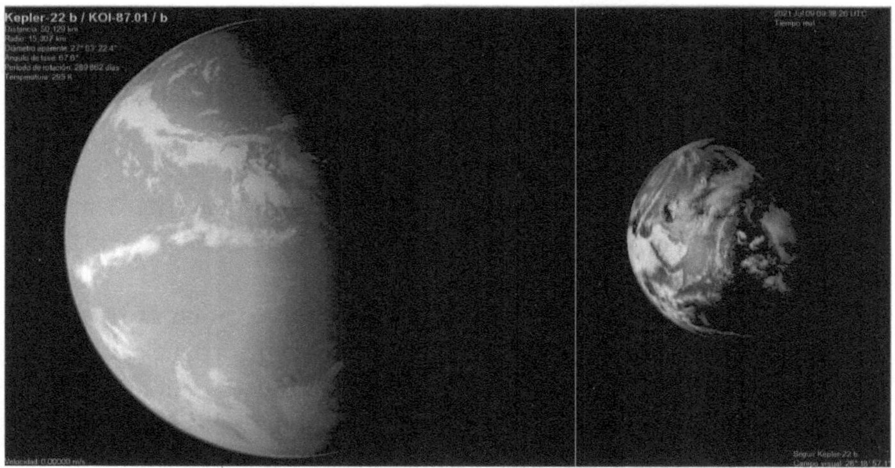

Kepler-22b: Closer to Finding an Earth (courtesy: NASA)

Despite the vast distance, the planet's presence captivates senses, inviting to explore its enigmatic landscape, adorned with vast stretches of azure-blue waters, reflecting the gentle glow of its distant sun. Kepler-22b orbits within the habitable zone of its parent star, Kepler-22, where conditions may be conducive to the presence of liquid water. This tantalizing possibility hints at the potential for oceans, rivers, and lakes teeming with life beneath the surface.

Discovered by NASA's Kepler Space Telescope, this distant world represents a triumph of scientific inquiry and human ingenuity. Standing before Kepler-22b, I am pondering the mysteries of existence and the vastness of the universe. In the grand tapestry of space and time, we are but a tiny speck, yet endowed with the ability to contemplate the cosmos and seek answers to age-old questions. Kepler-22b reminds of the boundless possibilities that await exploration and discovery beyond the confines of our own world.

At about 643 light-years from Earth, Betelgeuse also known as Alpha Orionis, the bright red star in the constellation of Orion, invites attention.

Betelgeuse stands out as one of the brightest stars in the constellation of Orion, marking the shoulder of the mighty hunter. Its fiery red hue contrasts vividly with the surrounding stars, making it an unmistakable celestial landmark. From our perspective on Earth, Betelgeuse shines proudly, beckoning observers to gaze upon its splendor.

It is a red supergiant, a class of star known for their immense size and brilliance. It dwarfs our own Sun, with a diameter estimated to be over 1,000 times larger. Its luminosity is equally staggering, with Betelgeuse shining tens of thousands of times brighter than the Sun.

This aging star has exhausted its core hydrogen fuel, causing it to swell and expand into a red supergiant. It will eventually meet its demise in a spectacular supernova explosion, enriching the cosmos with heavy elements forged in its fiery core.

As we observe Betelgeuse, we can notice the fluctuation of brightness over time. This variability adds to its mystique and intrigue, captivating astronomers for centuries. The exact cause of Betelgeuse's variability is still a subject of scientific inquiry, with theories ranging from pulsations in its outer layers to the presence of large, cool spots on its surface.

CHAPTER IX

Forty five minutes

As I advance curiously, between 12 minutes and 45 minutes of my journey, I encountered the Kepler planets which possibly can be home away from Earth once we're able to travel fast. Apart from this, there exist a few nebulae presenting a unique and fascinating view.

Located at about 1,200 light-years away in the constellation Lyra, as part of a multi-planet system potentially considerable habitable worlds orbit an orange-red dwarf star.

The planets Kepler-296e & Kepler-296f.

At about 1,400 light-years away, I see a large planet Kepler-1540b orbiting a sun-like star. It might have a thick atmosphere and conditions suitable for liquid water. The planet's sky must be dominated by its host star, shining brightly and providing ample warmth.

Positioned about 2,300 light-years away, Kepler-1652b is a super-Earth which could be rocky with a stable climate, illuminated by the steady light of its star. Its surface might support diverse ecosystems, with the potential for liquid water being high.

As I was lost in thoughts of the numerous Earth like exo-planets, the glimmering light from a star woke me up. The blue supergiant star Rigel aka Beta Orionis in the Orion constellation is one of the most luminous stars in our galaxy, radiating intense blue-white light. Located about 860 light years away from Earth, Rigel appears as a massive, glowing orb of intense blue-white light. The star's surface temperature exceeds 11,000 degrees Celsius (20,000 degrees Fahrenheit), causing it to radiate with a fierce, electric-blue hue. The light is so bright that it casts stark shadows across the surrounding interstellar space, illuminating nearby gas and dust clouds with a haunting, ethereal glow. It is around 70 times the radius of our Sun and emits tens of thousands of times more energy.

The star's surface roils with turbulent activity, as powerful stellar winds and magnetic fields create a dynamic and ever-changing facade. Standing here, I can almost feel the pulsations of energy emanating from its core, a reminder of the incredible nuclear fusion processes that power this stellar giant. In the distance, the majestic constellation of Orion frames Rigel, with its characteristic belt and other notable stars like Betelgeuse. Rigel serves as the 'foot' of Orion, anchoring the constellation in the celestial tapestry. The star's brilliance not only dominates the scene but also serves as a beacon, guiding the eye through the rich stellar landscape.

As I stand in awe, I am reminded that Rigel is not alone. It is part of a multiple star system, with smaller companion stars orbiting the supergiant. These companions, though not visible to the naked eye from Earth, add to the complexity and intrigue of this stellar region.

This reflection nebula associated with the star Rigel looks suspiciously like a fairytale crone. Formally known as IC 2118 in the constellation Orion, the Witch Head Nebula glows primarily by light reflected from the star. (courtesy: NASA)

The light from Rigel travels through the vastness of space, illuminating and interacting with distant nebulae. One such nebula, the Witch Head Nebula, lies nearby, its eerie blue glow reflecting Rigel's powerful light. The interplay of Rigel's brilliance with the surrounding cosmic dust and gas creates a scene of unparalleled beauty and wonder.

10 light years away from Rigel I could find another rocky exoplanet Kepler-1229b, appearing to have a stable climate possibly conducive to life.

Among the million blue celestial spheres, few notable names include Kepler-705b, Kepler-155c, Kepler-62f, Kepler-62e, Kepler-440b, Kepler-1544 b, Kepler-1410b, Kepler-442b, Kepler-174d, Kepler-283c, Kepler-452b, Kepler-1701b, Kepler-1653b, Kepler-443b and Kepler-1606b. From here, these planets appear as a potential Earth analog, with conditions that might support life. The light from their corresponding stars steadily warms, providing a temperate climate and there exists potential for liquid water too.

Messier 57 or M57 familiar as the Ring Nebula appeared as I leave behind the habitable zone of Lyra, in about 2,300 light-years away from Earth. The nebula is the remnant of a dying star that has shed its outer layers, leaving behind a core that will eventually become a white dwarf. From my vantage point, the Ring Nebula's intricate structure is clearly visible. The central region is filled with a diffuse, bluish glow, radiating outward and giving way to the striking ring of ionized gas that encircles it. The ring itself is composed of vibrant hues, ranging from soft greens to deep reds, each color representing different elements emitting light at specific wavelengths. The greenish-blue interior is primarily due to the emission from doubly ionized oxygen, while the outer regions glow red from the hydrogen gas. This colorful display is a testament to the powerful processes at work within the nebula, as intense ultraviolet radiation from the hot central star excites the surrounding gas, causing it to fluoresce.

As I gaze deeper into the heart of the Ring Nebula, the central white dwarf becomes apparent, though faint against the brilliant backdrop. This stellar remnant, once the core of a star similar to our Sun, is now a hot, dense object slowly cooling and fading over billions of years. Surrounding the main ring, the nebula's structure becomes more diffuse and faint, blending into the interstellar medium. The outer edges appear wispy and delicate, like tendrils of cosmic smoke, gradually dispersing into the surrounding space.

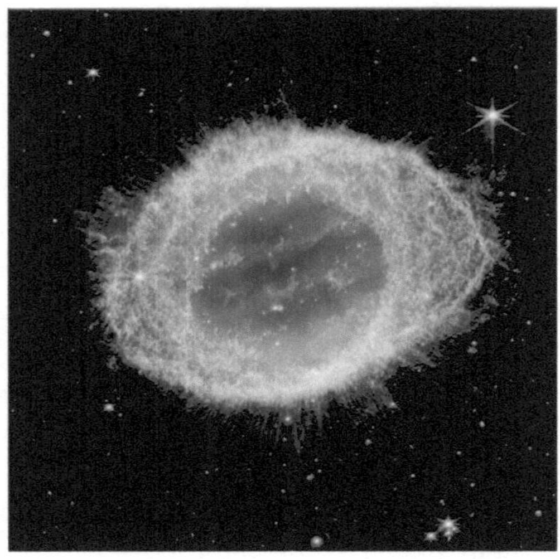

M57, or the Ring Nebula, is a planetary nebula, the glowing remains of a sun-like star. The tiny white dot in the center of the nebula is the star's hot core, called a white dwarf. (courtesy: NASA)

The Ring Nebula's 'human eye' shape and vivid colors make it a stunning spectacle, a beautiful yet poignant reminder of the life cycle of stars. The nebula's serene glow and intricate patterns are a stark contrast to the violent processes that created it, showcasing the delicate balance between creation and destruction in the cosmos.

The Ring Nebula, a fleeting yet breathtaking phenomenon, serves as a reminder of the transient beauty that exists throughout the galaxy.

CHAPTER X

Three hours

After travelling 7,000 light years, another celestial wonder stopped me. These are the iconic Pillars of Creation within the Eagle Nebula (M16). This serene region is a star birth site in the constellation of Serpens.

The towering tendrils of cosmic dust and gas sit at the heart of M16, or the Eagle Nebula. (courtesy: NASA)

I can see the interstellar clouds of gas and dust particles which are visually breathtaking and a vital area for star formation study. These ethereal towering Pillars of Creation are composed of dust and cool molecular hydrogen that are bathed in intense ultraviolet light and stellar winds from young scorching stars. As the name suggests, these are dense region where gas and dust collapses initiating the birth of protostars. Eventually these protostars will ignite nuclear fusion within their cores, thus becoming fully-fledged scintillating stars. But at the same I can see these beautiful pillars getting slowly eroded by the ultraviolet light coming from relatively nearer hot stars.

'Photoevaporation'. That's the name given to this process.

The detailed study of these Pillars and the enchanting Nebula has been made possible with advances in telescope technology. Images from Hubble Telescope were renowned for their exceptional clarity and details till they got superseded by those sent by JWST. Observations from the Spitzer Space Telescope unveils region of star formation that is shrouded by cosmic dust.

Thus, the Eagle Nebula and its Pillar of Creation continues being a symbol for continuous cycle of star birth and death, exemplifying the magnificence of stellar birth within the cosmos.

As I turn to look further apart, I'm mesmerized seeing the stellar majesty of Eta Carina. Located in the constellation of Carina is a binary system of two gargantuan stars. This celestial marvel is 7,500 light years from Earth and has been meticulously recorded by the generations of astronomers.

The binary system includes Eta Carina A, a Luminous Blue Variable (LBV), so titanic with mass about 100-150 times that of sun. Eta Carina B is massive O-type star with relatively lesser mass, around 30-80 solar masses.

The star system is coruscating, emitting light 5 million times than the Sun's light. One the most notal event in the Eta Carina's history is the Great Eruption which ejected large amount of material into space leading to the formation of a bipolar nebula. This is the Homunculus Nebula which is definitely one of the most striking features with this stellar system. This nebula consists of two large orange lobes of dust and gas which are expanding outward at the speed of 500-600 km/s providing a stunning visual spectacle.

Eta Carina A with its huge mass and instability is expected to end its life in a picturesque supernova. This explosion will release abundant energy that will outshine the entire Milky Way.

The ever changing present and the uncertain future of this celestial behemoth will keep the astronomical community enthralled.

35

CHAPTER XI

Six hours

After travelling for 6 hours of this amazing journey, I see a gigantic super-hot star, one of the largest known stars, Stephenson 2-18 (St2-18).

This is a remarkable red supergiant has its radius 2,150 times that of the Sun. It appears so enormous that if placed at the center of the solar system it would go beyond the orbit of Saturn.

Mesmerizing isn't it?

This extreme red hypergiant is located in the constellation of Scutum at about 19,000 light years away from the earth. It was identified from Stephenson 2 (St2) cluster, a group of red supergiant stars by an American astronomer Charles Bruce Stephenson.

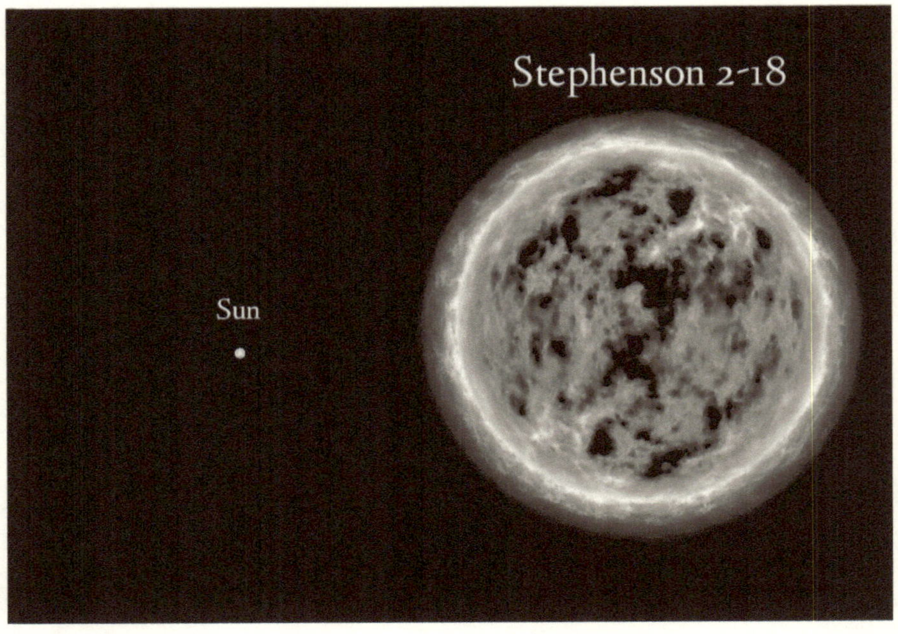

Sun & the hypergiant

Luminosity of Stephenson 2-18 is equally staggering which is about 440,000 times that of our Sun. With this luminosity and colossal size, it is one of the most glorious stellar objects studied in recent years. Studying it helps astronomers to understand the extent of stellar size and the physical and chemical processes happening in massive stars.

Recent studies reveal that Stephenson 2-18 is in its late stage of stellar evolution, expecting it to end its life in a core-collapse supernova dispersing heavy elements into the interstellar medium.

No doubt that Stars of our universe leaves any chance to blow our mind!

Slightly beyond this red super giant, I see a startling concentration of stars.

The Virgo Stellar Stream, also known as Virgo Overdensity is a dwarf spheroidal galaxy located in the halo of the Milky Way, in the Virgo Constellation.

This is the largest galaxy observable from earth based on the extent of the night sky it occupies. According to astronomers, this stellar stream is composed of older, metal-poor stars which are possibly the remnants of a dwarf galaxy or a globular cluster that has been cleaved by the Milky Way's gravitational force.

It was discovered in early 2000s by analyzing the photometric data from Sloan Digital Sky Survey (SDSS). By analyzing the motion and velocities of the stars of Virgo Stream, astronomers can map the distribution of the mysterious dark matter in the Milky Way. This is one of a consequential structure helping astronomers to understand the evolution of the Milky Way and its growth over time by accreting smaller satellite galaxies.

It is part of the larger population of stellar streams however, resembles the tidal stream produced by Sagittarius Dwarf Spheroidal galaxy.

Nearly at a distance of 30,000 light years from Earth, distributed over 90 square degrees of the sky, Virgo Stellar Stream is a splendid structure with darker matter featuring galactic cannibalism.

CHAPTER XII

Eight hours

Discovered by Bruce Balick and Robert Brown, Sagittarius A* (Sgr A*) is a supermassive black hole and a very compact astronomical radio source found at the Galactic centre of our Milky Way galaxy. It is nearly 26,000 light years away from our earth with its mass approximately 4 million times that of the Sun. After travelling at the speed one light year per second, it took us 8 hours to reach this enigmatic object.

Radio signals from the direction of the constellation Sagittarius, were detected by Karl Jansky fondly called as the fathers of radio astronomy, which with subsequent observations, done particularly in infrared and X-ray wavelengths confirmed that Sagittarius A* is the location of this supermassive black hole.

The event horizon of this super massive black hole has 17 times the diameter of our sun, which is nearly 24 million kilometres. Sagittarius A is shrouded by dense dust clouds which make it difficult to study this gigantic object from Earth. Hence, infrared telescopes are used to observe the motion of stars and gas surrounding it.

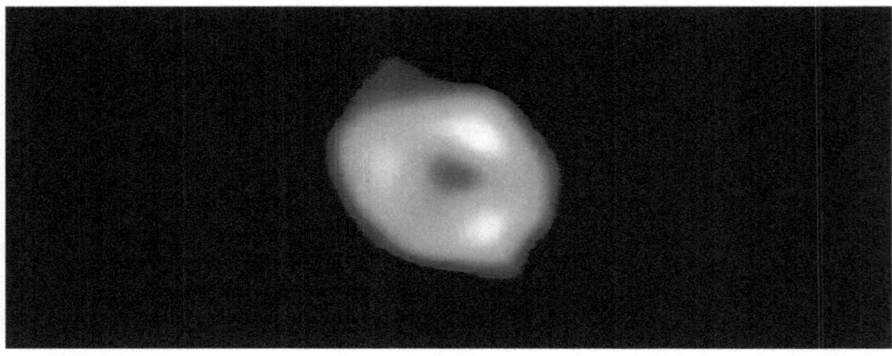

The power of multiple telescopes around the world was combined to capture the first image of the black hole at the center of our Milky Way, Sagittarius A (courtesy: NASA)*

A Star S2 revolves around Sagittarius A* in a highly elliptical orbit, bringing it very close to the black hole and providing us with some key information on the black hole's mass and gravitational influence.

Sagittarrius A* occasionally emits X-ray flares which are caused by rapid infall of material into it. On January 2015 these flares have been observed to be 400 times brighter than usual and were considered to be caused by the magnetic field entanglement of the gas flowing into the black hole. Astronomers have also observed molecular hydrogen-rich gas clouds and planet forming materials around Sagittarius A*.

Jets are produced by young stars and black holes when some material falling towards them is redirected outward. NASA's Chandra X-ray Observatory and National Science Foundation's Very Large Array (VLA) radio telescope confirms the production of jets of high-energy particles by Sgr A*.This study helped us understand the direction of the spin axis of Sgr A* which is parallel to the rotation axis of the Milky Way. However, presently Sgr A* is known to be consuming very little material, thus producing weak jets.

Observing such materials around the supermassive black hole helps us in understanding the accretion process and emission mechanism of the black hole. With the advancement in telescope technology like the upcoming Extremely Large Telescope (ELT), we'll be able to dive deep into the details of this mysterious object.

As I break the view and look around, another cosmic beauty caught my eye-The Canis Major Dwarf(CMa) which is the satellite galaxy of the Milky Way, also known as Canis Major Overdensity.

This is an irregular galaxy and one of our closest neighbour, harbouring high percentage of Red Giants. It lies at around 25,000light-years from Earth and 42,000 light years from galactic center, sharing sky with the Constellation Canis Major. This beauty is hidden by dense interstellar dust and gases in the disk of Milky Way.

It was only discovered in 2003 by a team led by Rodrigo Ibata, who analysed the datafrom Two-Micron All Sky Survey (2MASS). This was a collaborative astronomical mission which conducted an infrared survey allowing astronomers to peer through the layers of dustand detected a significant overdensity of class M stars (Red dwarf).

The mass of this dwarf galaxy is around billion solar masses which includes dark matter. In early 21st century Sloan Digital Sky Survey discovered that the Canis Major is being pulled by the gravitational field of

Milky Way Galaxy. This interaction causes CMa to lose stars thus results in the formation of complex ring like structure called Monoceros Ring which wraps itself around Milky Way three times. However, current theories suggest that this galaxy is accreted by the Milky Way.

NGC1851, NGC 2808, NGC 2298, NGC 1904 are the Globular clusters which orbits the center of Milky Way are thought to be part of Canis Major Dwarf before its accretion. Open clusters like Dolidze 25 and H18 are considered to be formed by the material deviated by the galaxy from the galactic center which also stimulated star formation. These clusters help astronomers to trace galaxy's interactions with Milky Way.

A recent study suggests that ripples in the Milky Way's stellar disk is result of Canis Major Dwarf galaxy merging with Milky Way. Today many studies doubts on the true nature of the overdensity and suggests that the trail of stars which could be part of warped galactic thin disk and thick disc population thus being a fascinating subject for astronomers to understand complex galactic interactions.

CHAPTER XIII

Two days

Two days past I left Earth, in search of infinity, I see the dynamic Twin Beacon of the Southern Sky, The Magellanic Clouds. This includes two irregular dwarf satellite galaxies of Milky Way, the Large Magellanic Cloud (LMC) and the Small Magellanic Cloud (SMC).

This galaxy lies in the constellation of Dorado with its center seen as a vibrant bar of stars surrounded by the disk of gas and dust which slowly dances and collapse forming new stars.

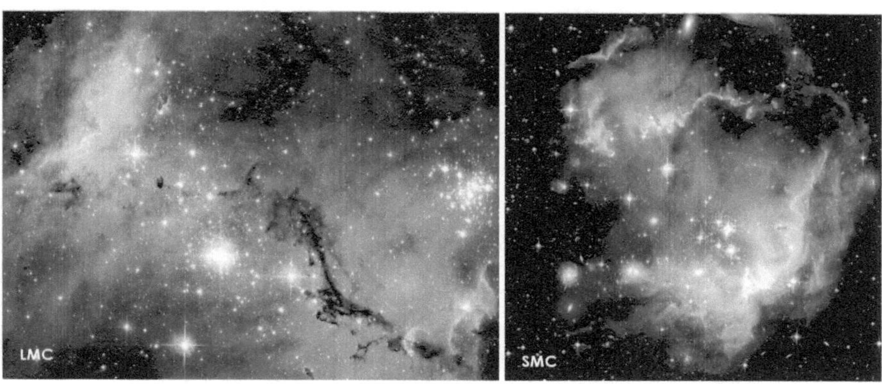

Large Magellanic Cloud, a satellite galaxy of the Milky Way, floats in space, in a long and slow dance around our galaxy. The tip of the "wing" of the Small Magellanic Cloud galaxy is dazzling in this view from NASA's Chandra X-ray Observatory, Hubble Space Telescope and Spitzer Space Telescope. (courtesy: NASA)

LMC is the fourth largest galaxy in the Local Group located approximately 163,000 light years away from the Earth. It is exceptionally lustrous with numerous star forming regions, with around 400 nebulae, 700 open clusters, 60 globular clusters accompanied with hundreds and thousands of blazing giant and supergiant stars.

An extraordinary region is alluring my attention. This is the Tarantula Nebula (30 Doradus), one of the most star-forming region in the Local

Group of galaxies. Tarantula Nebula excels as a celestial cradle harbouring vast number of young, hot, enormous stars which creates nebula's excellent glow. At the core of this nebula resides R136, clusters boasting its prodigious radiant stars.

Another huge blue supergiant in LMC, Sanduleak 202 underwent a cataclysmic supernova on February 24, 1987, shining so brilliantly that could be observed without any aid of telescope providing data on supernova mechanics.

On the other hand SMC is located 200,00 light years away from Earth and is named after the Portuguese explorer Ferdinand Magellan. This irregular galaxy looks like a hazy patch having clusters of young luminous stars and dust clouds though on a smaller scale than LMC.

I can see a vast bridge of gas connecting SMC with LMC. This is the Megallanic bridge which is a stream of neutral hydrogen and a star forming region. Despite being small, this dwarf galaxy is so bright that it can be seen to the unaided eyes from the Southern Hemisphere and near Equator.

Recent observations from NASA's Chandra X-Ray Observatory have detected X-ray emission from young stars of this diminutive galaxy. Thus, providing an opportunity to investigate phenomena that are challenging to observe in galaxies farther away. Its proximity to LCM leads to an intricate interplay of gravitational forces, therfore influencing this dynamics of both the galaxies.

This neighbour twin continues to be a cornerstone for cosmic understanding, thereby enhancing our comprehension of the universe's large-scale structure

CHAPTER XIV

One month

After travelling for a month with the speed of one light year per second, I have encountered a galaxy twice as the size of Milky Way.

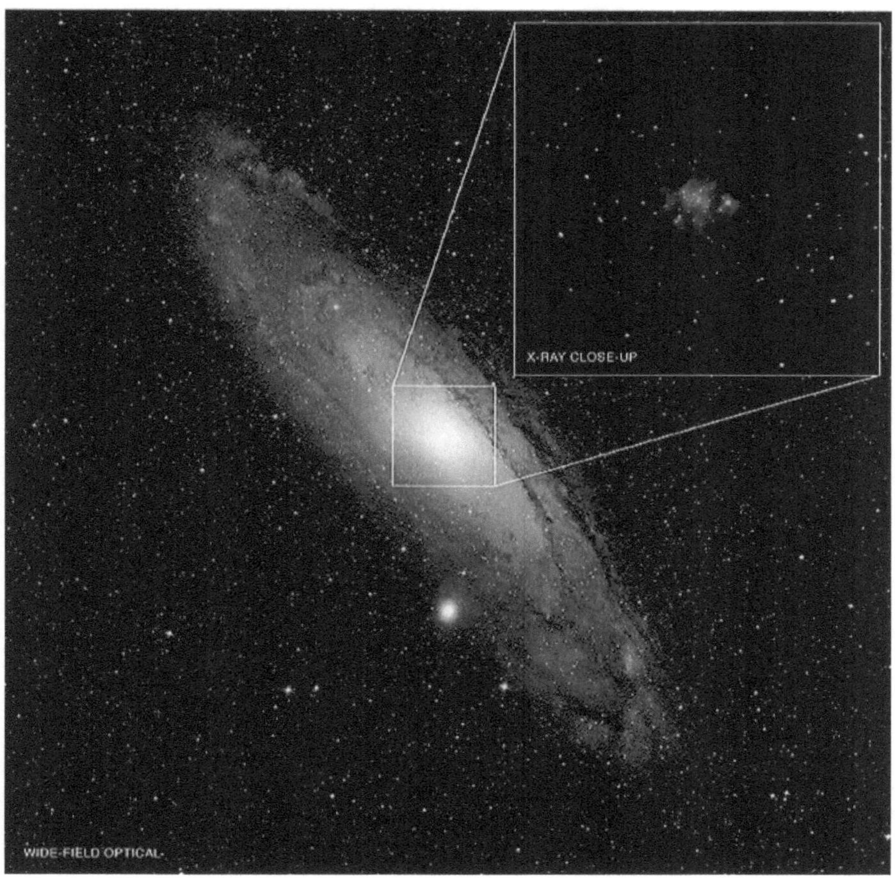

A wide-field view of Andromeda, with an inset containing X-ray data from multiple observations of the central region. (courtesy: NASA)

This is the renowned Andromeda Galaxy also known as M31 (Messier 31), located in the Andromeda constellation. It is the most distant object that can be seen with naked eyes from the Earth and is located at around 2.5 light years.

This galactic neighbour is a magnificent spiral galaxy and the largest galaxy in the 'local group' harboring trillions of stars. Gravitational influence of Andromeda encompasses satellite galaxies like M32, M110 and around 460 densely populated globular clusters. These satellites are elliptical dwarf galaxies offering valuable insights on merger events in history.

It appears lighter in mass than Milky Way from where I stand and has got a central bulge fenced by the disk of stars with several spiral arms. I can see a ring of dust which seems comparatively colder dust and debris. I remember the report of the Herschel mission by European Space Agency which observed longer wavelength infrared light that revealed these ring of cold dust ranges in temperature near tens of the degree above absolute zero.

Meanwhile, the central region were new stars are born appears to have warmer dust.

From far away distance, I can visualize our galaxy approaching towards Andromeda and these are on a collision course, which may happen in about 4.5 billion years.

I wonder the name of the child born out of mating Andromeda with Milky Way. It can be called 'Milkomeda' or 'Milkdromeda' or even 'Andro Way'.

Star jokes!

This collision event will offer a unique opportunity for the astronomers to understand long term effects on galactic structure and evolution, but will the planet Earth remain inhabited then is a question. We may migrate to some newer galaxy and witness a glimpse of our galactic future in the cosmic landscape.

Imagination has no limits.

As I stand pondering into the luminosity magnitude of such a collision, another captivating view of a spiral galaxy took my eyes away.

The Triangulum Galaxy is also known as M33 (Messier 33). Its well defined spiral structure with several prominent arms exhibiting signs of its interaction with the nearby galaxies, reminds of a hungry octopus.

This gigantic image of the Triangulum Galaxy — also known as Messier 33 — is a composite of about 54 different pointings with Hubble's Advanced Camera for Surveys. With a staggering size of 34,372 times 19,345 pixels, it is the second-largest image ever released by Hubble. (courtesy: NASA)

Floating at around 2.73 million light years away from Earth, housing around 40 billion stars, It is the third largest galaxy in the 'Local Group'. However, M33 is relatively luminous with magnitude of 5.7 thus can be observed with unaided eyes from planet Earth. The star formation rate of Triangulum galaxy is nearly ten times more intense than the Andromeda galaxy as per the observations done by the Hubble Space Telescope.

I noticed a bright blue patch in the galaxy. This is designated as NGC 604, the largest star forming region of M33. Other than this it also hosts numerous H II regions where new stars are born, highlighting its active stellar nursery status.

Triangulum galaxy is also gravitationally interacting with the Andromeda galaxy similar to Milky Way - Andromeda, which can lead to another impending collision thus shaping the intricacies of new worlds.

Three months

Three Months past leaving Earth in the expedition of the infinite Universe, a distinctive structure made me take a halt and look around. Centaurus A, also known as NGC 5128 galaxy, located about 13 million light-years away from Solar system which is unusual in its appearance due to the presence of dark band of dust that cuts across its luminous core. This dust lane, a remnant of a cosmic collision between a spiral and an elliptical galaxy, creates a dramatic contrast against the bright, elliptical glow of the galaxy.

Centaurus A is the fifth brightest galaxy in the sky — making it an ideal target for amateur astronomers. This image was made using data from the Hubble, Spitzer, and Chandra space telescopes and the Very Large Array. (courtesy: NASA)

Keenly observing, at the heart of Centaurus A, I can see the brilliant core powered by a supermassive black hole, emitting intense radiation and high-energy jets that extend far into space.

These jets, composed of particles moving at nearly the speed of light, illuminate the surrounding interstellar medium, creating a vivid display of cosmic activity. Surrounding the core and dust lane, the galaxy's halo glows softly, filled with countless stars and globular clusters.

Standing here, I feel the immense scale and dynamic nature of Centaurus A. Its blend of cosmic collision remnants and active galactic core offers a fascinating glimpse into the complex and powerful processes that shape galaxies.

Another few days of journey away from Centaurus A, I see another stunning spiral galaxy known as Sculptor Galaxy or NGC 253. It appears tilted towards me, giving a magnificent view of its intricate spiral structure. The spiral arms are dotted with pinkish regions of star formation, known as H II regions, where new stars are being born in clouds of hydrogen gas.

The intricate patterns in the arms and the core that contrast with the bright starlight, appears as if a snake crawls up to the core. These are dust lanes weave through the arms and the core, composed of interstellar dust, absorbing and scattering the light from the stars behind them, which gives the galaxy a textured, almost three-dimensional appearance, crediting some unknown sculptor for the 11 million light-years away beauty.

The overall light of the galaxy is a soft bluish-white, a mix of the young, hot stars in the spiral arms and the older, cooler stars in the core. This blend of light creates a serene, yet dynamic, scene as the galaxy slowly rotates, its arms trailing behind in a grand cosmic dance.

Such elegance and complexity reminds me of John Keats who wrote "A thing of beauty is a joy forever".

Surrounding the galaxy, a faint halo of older stars and globular clusters can be seen, adding to the galaxy's grandeur. These clusters are ancient, some as old as the galaxy itself, and they orbit the galaxy like silent sentinels, preserving the history of its formation and evolution.

Slightly far, off the shoulders of Sculptor galaxy, another graceful beauty, the M81 or Messier 81 galaxy fondly known as Bode's Galaxy shines bright. Located about 12 million light-years away from planet Earth, in the constellation Ursa Major constellation, Bode's Galaxy is a splendid example of a grand design spiral galaxy.

This central bulge is home to older, cooler stars, whose combined light creates a brilliant, concentrated center. From this luminous heart, the spiral arms of M81 unfurl in a stunning display. These arms wind outwards in a symmetrical, pinwheel pattern, highlighted by dark lanes of interstellar dust that trace the spiral structure. The regions of star formation, marked by the glowing clouds of ionized gas, add splashes of pink and red, indicating areas where new stars are being born.

As I take in the view, the overall symmetry and elegance of Bode's Galaxy stand out. The spiral arms are well-defined and evenly spaced, giving the galaxy a sense of balance and harmony. The interplay of colors—from the golden core to the blue spiral arms and the pink star-forming regions—creates a vivid and dynamic scene.

In the background, the faint glow of countless more distant galaxies can be seen, providing a cosmic context to M81's grandeur. The galaxy's proximity to its companion, the irregular galaxy M82 (the Cigar Galaxy), is also noteworthy. Together, they form a striking pair, interacting gravitationally and affecting each other's structure and star formation activity.

CHAPTER XVI

Ten months

As I stand here, the mesmerizing beauty of the Whirlpool Galaxy, also known as Messier 51 (M51) pushes me to ponder on the mysteries that lie within. Located approximately 23 million light-years away in the constellation Canes Venatici, this stunning celestial spectacle captivates with its swirling arms of stars and dust.

In M51, these arms serve as star-formation factories, compressing hydrogen gas and creating clusters of new stars. (courtesy: NASA)

With a diameter spanning over 60,000 light-years, the Whirlpool Galaxy is a grand design spiral galaxy, a celestial masterpiece sculpted by the forces of gravity and stellar evolution. Its graceful spiral arms, adorned with bright knots of young, hot blue stars and vast lanes of cosmic dust, draw us deeper into its cosmic embrace.

At the heart of this celestial whirlpool lies a dramatic dance of cosmic proportions. A supermassive black hole lurks amidst the galactic center, its immense gravitational pull sculpting the galaxy's structure and influencing the motion of stars and gas around it. This gravitational interplay gives rise to the swirling patterns and dynamic beauty that adorn the Whirlpool Galaxy.

Intriguingly, the Whirlpool Galaxy is not alone in this cosmic ballet. Interacting with its smaller companion galaxy, NGC 5195, the two engage in a celestial dance, their gravitational tango resulting in the stunning interaction seen before us. Streams of gas and dust bridge the gap between the two galaxies, evidence of their gravitational embrace.

The Sombrero Galaxy, also known as Messier 104 (M104) resides approximately 28 million light-years away in the constellation Virgo, adorning the cosmos with its grandeur. Its distinctive morphology immediately captures the observer's attention—a bright, bulging core surrounded by a vast, dark dust lane that wraps around its equatorial region, resembling the brim of a 'Sombrero hat'. This iconic feature lends the galaxy its name and adds to its mystique.

As I continue to observe, the gaze is drawn to the radiant nucleus at the heart of the galaxy—a dense congregation of stars, gas, and dust, where intense stellar activity ignites the space around it. The brilliance emanating from this central region contrasts sharply with the shadowy band of dust that encircles it, creating a captivating interplay of light and shadow. Stretching outward from the nucleus, graceful spiral arms adorned with clusters of young, luminous stars spiral outward in a mesmerizing dance, painting the cosmic canvas with intricate patterns of light and shadow. These spiral arms, adorned with countless stellar nurseries and star-forming regions, weave a tapestry of celestial beauty across the vast reaches of space.

CHAPTER XVII

Two years

I have reached about 53 million light-years away from Earth.

I am amazed to feel like having a million fireflies around me, as am standing mesmerized in front of the Messier 87 (aka M87), a giant elliptical galaxy in the Virgo Cluster.

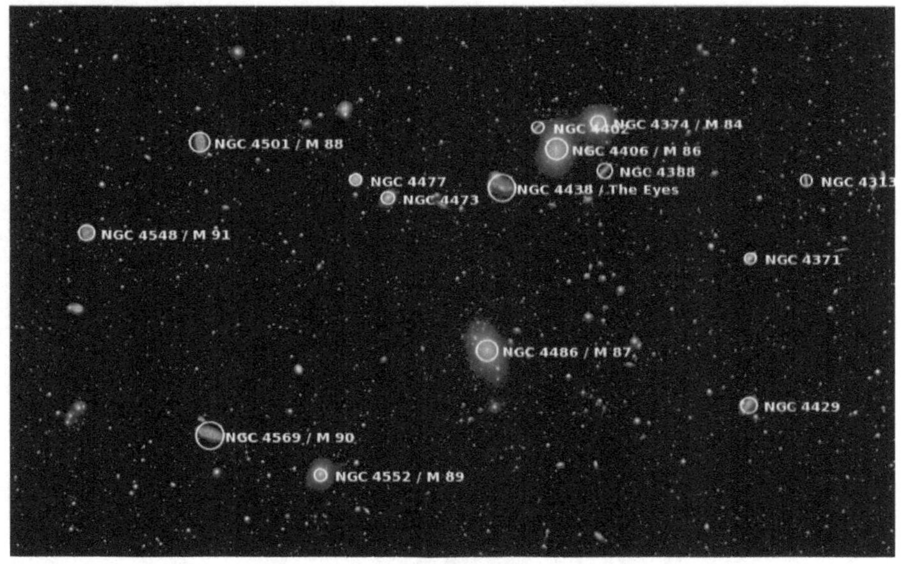

A mosaic of telescopic images showing the central region of the Virgo Cluster lingering above the plane of our Milky Way galaxy. (courtesy: NASA)

Unlike other spiral galaxies, M87 lacks the elegant, winding arms of spirals and instead presents a more rounded, almost featureless glow. The galaxy's vast, diffuse light stretches out into the surrounding darkness, tapering off into a faint halo that hints at its immense scale. This smooth, spherical shape is a hallmark of elliptical galaxies, which are composed mainly of older, redder stars.

At the heart of M87 lies its most captivating feature. Yes, it is a supermassive black hole, one of the most massive known, with a mass equivalent to several billion suns. This black hole was famously imaged by the Event Horizon Telescope once, providing the first direct visual evidence of a black hole's event horizon. Another surprise came to me as the jet of the high-energy particles that is being ejected from the vicinity of this black hole. This relativistic jet, which extends thousands of light-years into space, appears as a bright, narrow beam of light, a testament to the incredible energy and dynamic processes occurring at the galaxy's core.

Streaming out from the center of M87 like a cosmic searchlight is one of nature's most amazing phenomena: a black-hole-powered jet of subatomic particles traveling at nearly the speed of light. (courtesy: NASA)

Surrounding the bright central region, the galaxy's light is scattered with numerous globular clusters, like tiny, dense swarms of stellar population – giving the feel of fireflies again.

As I stand wondering over the predominantly golden light compared to the blue, star-forming regions of spiral galaxies, I remember the lectures of *Arun* about the age of galaxies and the colour of light from them. As per him, as galaxies age to advanced stages, they sent out yellowish hue rather than the young blue stellar population. This mature starlight tells a story of a galaxy that has long since ceased forming new stars, instead living out the later stages of its evolution.

Watching this marvel, I am reminded of its significant place in our understanding of the universe. Its supermassive black hole, the relativistic jet, and its status as a giant elliptical galaxy all make M87 a focal point for studying galaxy formation, evolution, and the behavior of black holes. The galaxy's ancient stars and the halo of dark matter that envelopes it further intrigue, suggesting a long and complex history stretching back to the early universe.

M87, in all its grandiosity, serves as a window into the distant past and a beacon for future astronomical discoveries.

Standing here and observing the vastness, I feel a profound sense of connection to the cosmos. The light from such galaxies has traveled across the vast expanse of space for millions of years to reach our Earth, a journey that underscores the vastness and age of the universe.

Walking among the spectacular galaxies of Virgo Cluster, another elegant distant object pulled my curious eye – the NGC 2770 spiral galaxy in the constellation Lynx. It lies at about 88 million light-years away from Earth showcasing the timeless beauty of the cosmos.

The core, densely packed with stars, emits a soft, warm glow, contrasting with the cooler, and more diffuse light of the spiral arms. The arms themselves are adorned with countless stars, clusters, and regions of interstellar gas and dust, forming a delicate pattern that speaks to the ongoing processes of star formation and evolution.

NGC 2770 has earned the nickname 'Supernova Factory' due to the remarkable number of supernovae observed within it. As I reach closer to the galaxy, I can imagine the powerful supernova explosions that have occurred here, leaving behind remnants that blend into the galactic structure. These cataclysmic events, where massive stars end their lives in brilliant explosions, have punctuated the galaxy's history, briefly outshining the entire galaxy each time they occur. Unlike M87, the light from this galaxy is a mix of the young, hot, blue stars scattered along the spiral arms and the older, cooler, yellow and red stars that populate the central bulge.

Filled with awe and curiosity, I am wondering about such galaxies those holds countless mysteries and stories waiting to be uncovered, each one a testament to the grandeur and complexity of the Universe.

CHAPTER XVIII

Fifteen years

Fifteen years into the journey, at the speed of one light year per second, I have come out of a spectacular structure with million branches, sharp contrasts, stark shadows, and vivid clarity and intense illumination.

It's Laniakea Supercluster.

Before me, lies a tapestry of billions of stars and countless galaxies, each a shimmering island in the dark ocean of space. The supercluster's intricate web-like structure is a testament to the forces of gravity and dark matter that have sculpted it over billions of years. I can see the dense clusters of galaxies, like the Virgo Cluster, acting as the anchor points in this vast network. These clusters are connected by long, thin filaments of galaxies, resembling the threads of a cosmic spiderweb.

Laniakea Supercluster of galaxies contains thousands of galaxies that includes our Milky Way Galaxy, the Local Group of galaxies, and the entire nearby Virgo Cluster of Galaxies. (computer-generated visualization)

As I gaze upon the vast expanse of the Laniakea Supercluster, I am awe-struck by the sheer scale and grandeur of this cosmic structure. Stretching across 520 million light-years, Laniakea is a colossal assembly of galaxies, clusters, and cosmic filaments that forms a gravitationally bound region of the universe. The name 'Laniakea', which means "immense heaven" in Hawaiian, perfectly encapsulates the awe-inspiring nature of this supercluster.

The heart of Laniakea is the 'Great Attractor', a gravitational anomaly that draws galaxies toward it with incredible force. This region is shrouded in mystery, as the dense concentration of galaxies and dark matter exerts a powerful gravitational pull, influencing the motion of everything within the supercluster.

As I continue to explore, I notice the diversity of galaxies that populate Laniakea. Spiral galaxies, with their elegant, winding arms, rotate gracefully, while elliptical galaxies, more amorphous and older, sit like ancient guardians of the cosmos. Irregular galaxies add to the variety, their chaotic shapes hinting at turbulent pasts filled with cosmic collisions and interactions.

The light from these galaxies takes millions, even billions of years to reach Earth even to offer a glimpse into the distant past. It is a humbling reminder of the vastness of space and the immense timescales over which the universe evolves.

Laniakea is not an isolated structure; it is part of an even larger network known as the 'cosmic web'. This web connects superclusters across the universe, forming the large-scale structure of the cosmos. Beyond the boundaries of Laniakea, other superclusters like the Shapley Supercluster and the Perseus-Pisces Supercluster continue the grand pattern of cosmic architecture.

Standing here, absorbing the grandeur of Laniakea, I am filled with a profound sense of wonder and curiosity. This supercluster is a testament to the beauty and complexity of the universe, a vast and interconnected structure that stretches the limits of human understanding and imagination.

CHAPTER XIX

Twenty five years

57

Beauty of the Universe never stops surprising.

A quater century long peregrination brings me to 600 million light years from Earth.

My eyes widened in wonder, drinking in the endless parade of picturesque creations.

I stand before Cygnus A, the most powerful radio galaxy in the constellation Cygnus. I can see the bright central core of this galaxy, which is home to a supermassive black hole. This black hole, millions of times the mass of our Sun, is the engine driving the intense activity here.

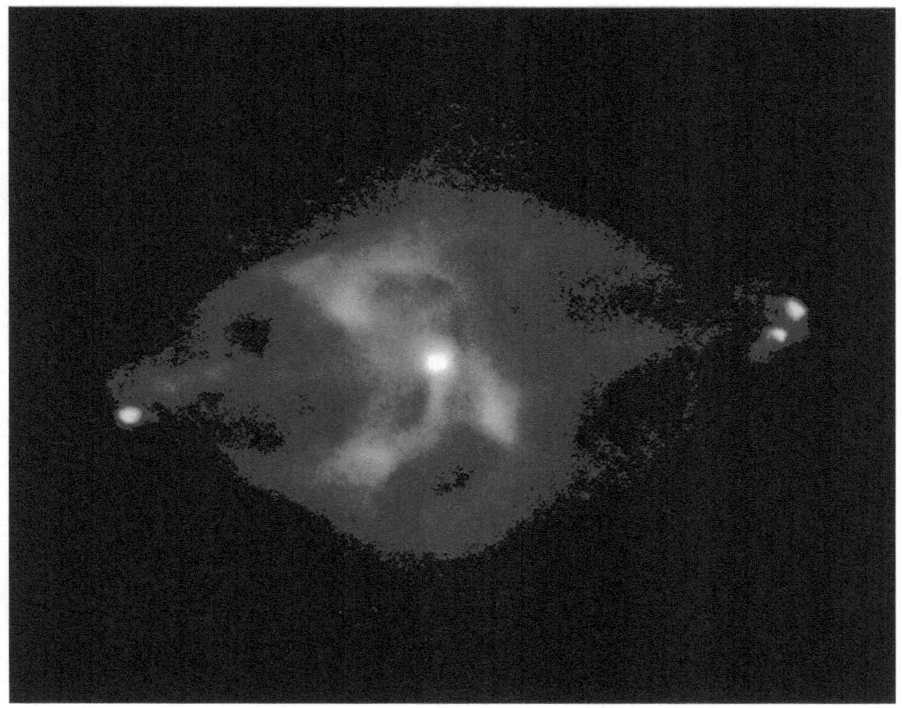

X-ray image of Cygnus A showing giant bubble filled with hot x-ray emitting gas (blue). (courtesy: NASA)

Around the core, an accretion disk of gas and dust spirals inward, emitting enormous amounts of energy as it heats up. This energy manifests in the form of intense radio waves, which are among the brightest in the entire sky. The sight of Cygnus A is dominated by two colossal jets of relativistic particles that shoot out from the poles of the black hole at nearly the speed of light. These jets extend millions of light-years into space, forming vast lobes on either side of the galaxy.

The jets are not just beams of light but are filled with high-energy particles that interact with the intergalactic medium, creating shock waves and radio emissions that are detectable from Earth. These radio lobes glow vividly in the radio spectrum, revealing a structure that dwarfs the optical galaxy itself.

As I focus on the central region of Cygnus A, I'm captivated by the complexities of the surrounding gas and dust. The intricate patterns and structures within the jets and lobes are a testament to the powerful and dynamic processes at play. The interplay of gravity, magnetic fields, and high-energy physics creates a mesmerizing spectacle that is both beautiful and scientifically fascinating.

Seeing Cygnus A in this detail, I am reminded of the immense power that galaxies can wield and the profound impact of supermassive black holes on their environments. Cygnus A stands as a beacon of radio light in the universe, a cosmic lighthouse illuminating the vast expanse of space with its incredible energy.

CHAPTER XX

Four hundred and fifty years

It's been 450 years of this incredible journey!

Now I can see these far-flung luminescent galaxies offering tantalizing glimpse into the depths of the universe's infancy.

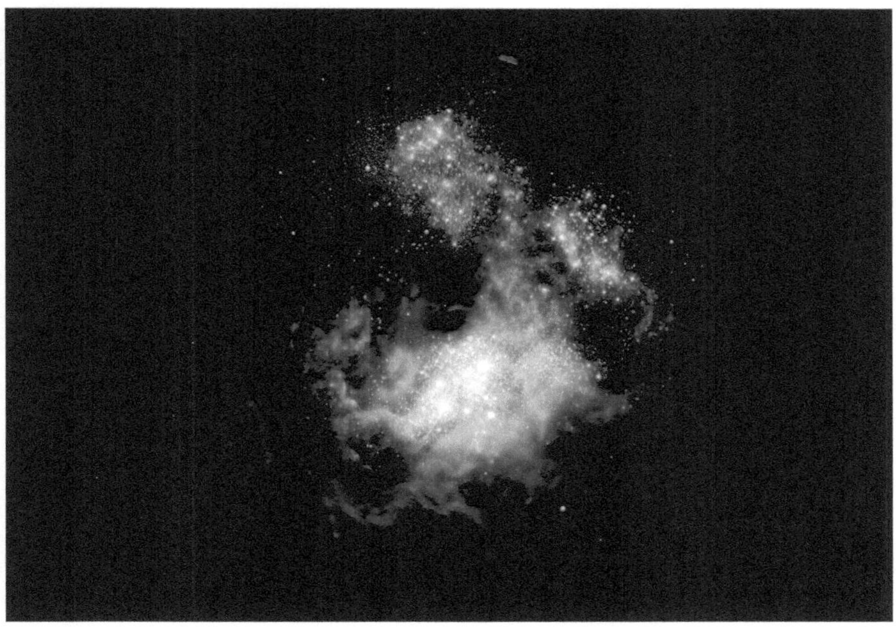

Artist's impression of CR7 the brightest galaxy in the early Universe (courtesy: European Southern Observatory)

One of these is the Cosmos Redshift 7 (CR7) located 12.9 billion years away from Earth yet shining so brilliantly with its brightness 10 trillion times more than Sun. This characteristic feature makes it one of the most distant galaxies ever observed. It is also known as high redshift Lyman-alpha emitter galaxy. Its discovery was made using Subaru and Keck telescopes by a team led by David Sobral in Hawaii. This lucent galaxy shows strong evidence of first generation stars i.e. Population III stars which are seen as a bright pocket of blue stars and the rest of the galaxy accommodating redder Population II stars.

CR7 is featuring its several luminous areas, each containing large star-forming regions. These are Lyman-alpha blobs, which are believed to be energized by the radiation from massive young stars of this primeval galaxy.

Towards my right I see another remarkable galaxy, JADES-GS-Z13-0. It is a high redshift Lyman-break galaxy, one of the most recent discoveries by the JWST during NIRCam imaging on 29 September 2022.

JADES-GS-z13-0 is situated in the Great Observatories Origins Deep Survey – South (GOODS-S) area within the constellation Fornax, encompassing the Hubble Ultra Deep Field, around 13.1 billion light years away from Earth.

These distant galaxies unravel the mysteries of the early universe, by providing crucial data to refine models of cosmic evolution.

CHAPTER XXI

Six hundred years

Massive!

That's the adjective which comes to mind as I see this giant.

Its 'Tonantzintla', another gargantuan black hole!

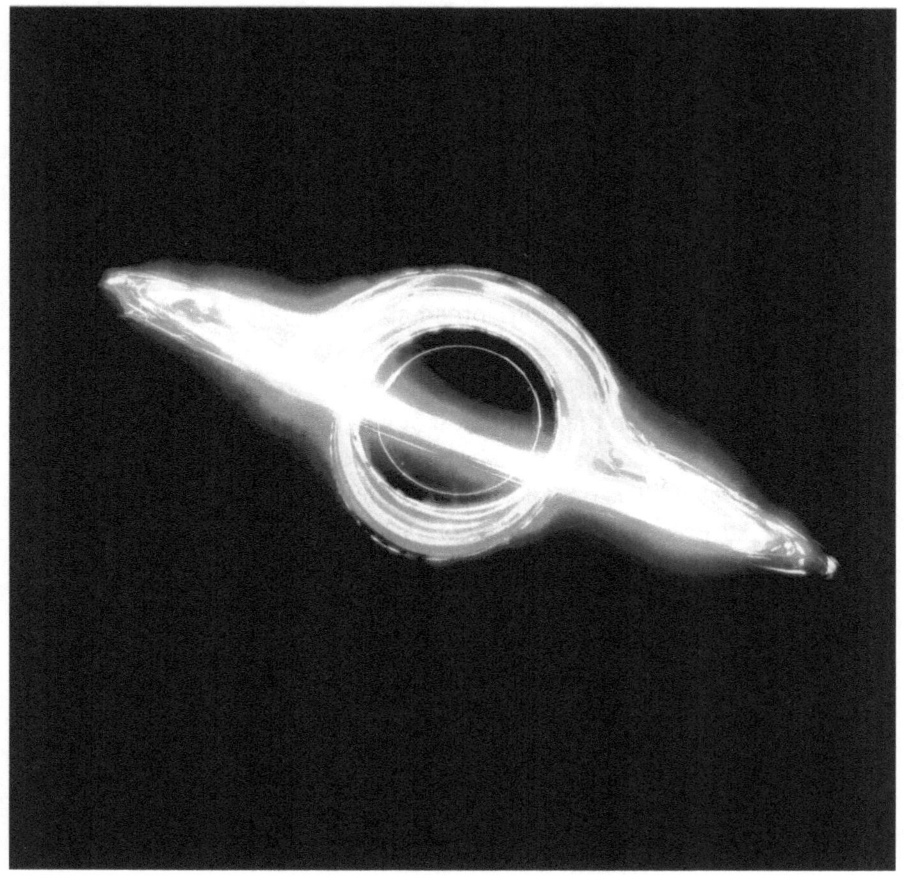

Artist's conception of Tonantzintla (courtesy: Pablo Carlos Budassi)

This is larger than the orbit of planet Neptune in our solar system. Yes it is a gigantesque 130 billion kilometers across.

We earthlings are relatively newer animals as the big bang happened not in very far history. It is difficult to explain how a black hole of such colossal size could have formed in the comparably short elapsed duration since the big bang.

During 1957, two Mexican astronomers Braulio Iriarte and Enrique Chavira, on observing through the Schmidt telescope at the Tonantzintla Observatory in Mexico, entered the number 618 in the ledger, thus naming this violet quasar.

The might of 'Tonantzintla 618' aka 'Ton 618' makes all adjectives ineffective. Its mere existence definitely is a challenge to the celebrated theories of black hole growth. Traversing a commoving distance of nearly 18.2 billion light-years from home, I now stand before an extremely luminous Quasar which is 66 billion times heavier than that of our Sun. Its gleaming accretion disc, which is brighter than the entire 400 billion stars shining together in the Milky Way galaxy, is blinding the most of the 'Canes Venatici constellation' (Latin for *hunting dogs*).

Located near the border of the constellations Canes Venatici and Coma Berenices, 618 is a hyperluminous, broad-absorption-line, radio-loud quasar and Lyman-alpha blob.

Bologna, in Italy during the 1970s has witnessed numerous discoveries about 618, among which the distinction of it as a quasar observing the radio emission stands significant. Later Marie-Helene Ulrich studied the emission lines and designated it as one of the most luminous quasars known.

It is not surprising that such elephantine black holes have significant roles in formation of galaxies and in shaping the universe.

Awe-inspired by the magnitude of infinity, I am remembering Robert Lee Frost's poem 'Stopping by woods on a snowy evening' which said;
"The woods are lovely, dark and deep,
But I have promises to keep
And miles to go before I sleep
And miles to go before I sleep".

Epilogue – Edge Of The Observable Universe

Thousands of galaxies flood this near-infrared image of galaxy cluster SMACS 0723. High-resolution imaging from NASA's James Webb Space Telescope combined with a natural effect known as gravitational lensing made this finely detailed image possible. (courtesy: NASA)

Standing at the edge of the observable universe, it's definitely overwhelming by the sheer magnitude and profound beauty of the cosmos stretched out before me. Here, at the very limits of what we can see, the universe reveals it's most ancient and distant secrets, a tapestry woven with the light of countless galaxies, some of which have traveled for over 13 billion years to reach this point.

Looking back, the view is a deep, cosmic expanse filled with faint, shimmering galaxies, their light a relic of an era close to the beginning of time itself. Each galaxy, a collection of billions of stars, planets, and possibly even life, appears as tiny, luminous specks scattered across the dark canvas of space. The light from these galaxies is redshifted, stretched to longer, redder wavelengths by the expansion of the universe, painting the distant cosmos in hues of red and infrared.

Around us, the cosmic microwave background forms a nearly uniform glow, the afterglow of the Big Bang. This faint radiation, the oldest light observable, bathes the universe in subtle, pervasive warmth, a silent echo of the universe's fiery birth. The cosmic microwave background is a testament to the universe's origins, a reminder of the moment when the cosmos transitioned from opaque, hot plasma to a transparent, star-filled expanse.

The vast emptiness of intergalactic space is punctuated by the occasional bright flash of distant quasars and gamma-ray bursts, powerful beacons that momentarily outshine entire galaxies. These energetic phenomena hint at the dynamic and sometimes violent processes shaping the universe even in its most remote corners.

Beyond this boundary, the light from more distant regions has not yet had time to reach us, and thus remains forever hidden from view. The observable universe, though immense, is but a small fraction of the entire cosmos, its edge a horizon beyond which lie unknown realms.

The sense of scale is staggering, and we will feel a profound connection to the universe and its history. Each photon that reaches this boundary carries with it a story, a whisper of events that occurred billions of years ago, long before the Earth formed and life began. Here, at the edge of the observable universe, we're both spectators to the grandeur of the cosmos and participants in its ongoing story, a tiny part of a vast, interconnected whole.

This vantage point offers a humbling perspective on our place in the universe. It is a reminder of the incredible journey that light undertakes to traverse the cosmos and of the boundless mysteries that lie beyond our current understanding.

Standing at this cosmic edge, we should be humbled, filled with awe and wonder, inspired by the beauty and complexity of the universe that surrounds us.

Glossary Of Astronomy

- **Accretion Disk:** A structure formed by the gravitational attraction of material, such as gas, dust, and other debris, swirling around a central object, typically a star, black hole, or young stellar object.
- **Active Galactic Nucleus (AGN):** The central region of a galaxy that emits unusually high amounts of radiation across the electromagnetic spectrum, often powered by accretion onto a supermassive black hole.
- **Astronomical Unit (AU):** Unit of length used in astronomy to measure distances within the solar system. It is defined as the average distance between the Earth and the Sun, approximately 149.6 million kilometers (about 93 million miles). The AU serves as a convenient reference for describing the orbits of planets, asteroids, comets, and other objects in our solar system. It provides a scale that allows astronomers to easily compare and understand the relative distances between celestial bodies across the Universe.
- **Black Hole:** A region of space-time where gravity is so strong that nothing, not even light, can escape.
- **Brown Dwarf:** Objects having size between that of a giant planet like Jupiter and that of a small star. In fact, most astronomers would classify any object with between 15 times the mass of Jupiter and 75 times the mass of Jupiter to be a brown dwarf.
- **Celestial Sphere:** Imaginary sphere of arbitrarily large radius centered on the Earth, onto which all celestial objects are projected for the purposes of locating and tracking them.
- **Chandra X-ray Observatory:** Launched in 1999, the Chandra X-ray Observatory observes the universe in X-ray wavelengths. It has provided valuable insights into phenomena such as black holes, supernovae remnants, and galaxy clusters.
- **Cosmic Dust:** Also known as interstellar dust, is a key component of the space between stars in galaxies. It consists of tiny solid particles, typically ranging in size from a few nanometers to several micrometers. These particles are composed of various materials, including silicates, carbon compounds, ices, and metals.
- **Cosmic Inflation:** A theory in cosmology that proposes a period of extremely rapid exponential expansion of the universe immediately

following the Big Bang. This brief but intense expansion is thought to have occurred within the first tiny fraction of a second after the universe came into existence.

- **Cosmic Microwave Background (CMB):** The residual radiation left over from the Big Bang, filling the universe uniformly.
- **Cosmic Microwave Background Radiation:** The CMB radiation is the afterglow of the Big Bang, providing a snapshot of the universe when it was just 380,000 years old.
- **Cosmic rays:** High-energy particles that originate from sources outside the solar system and travel through space at nearly the speed of light. They consist mainly of protons, atomic nuclei, and electrons, although they can also include heavier atomic nuclei, such as helium, carbon, and iron.
- **Cosmic Scale Factor:** The cosmic scale factor quantifies the expansion of the universe over time. As the universe evolves, the scale factor $a(t)$ increases, indicating that distances between galaxies, clusters, and other cosmic structures are growing.
- **Cosmic Web:** The large-scale structure of the universe composed of interconnected filaments of galaxies and voids.
- **Dark Energy:** A mysterious force that is causing the expansion of the universe to accelerate.
- **Dark Matter:** A form of matter that does not emit, absorb, or reflect light, but is inferred to exist due to its gravitational effects on visible matter.
- **Doppler Effect:** Change in frequency or wavelength of a wave in relation to an observer who is moving relative to the wave source. It applies to all types of waves, including sound, light, and electromagnetic waves.
- **Elliptical Galaxy:** A type of galaxy with a smooth, ellipsoidal shape and little to no spiral structure composed mainly of older stars.
- **ESPRESSO instrument on Very Large Telescope:** A cutting-edge spectrograph designed for high-precision radial velocity measurements of celestial objects.
- **Event Horizon:** The event horizon is a boundary in spacetime beyond which events cannot affect an outside observer. It is most commonly associated with black holes, where it represents the point of no return: anything that crosses the event horizon is inevitably drawn into the black hole's singularity and cannot escape.
- **Exoplanet:** A planet that orbits a star outside of our solar system.

- **Fermi Gamma-ray Space Telescope:** Launched in 2008, the Fermi Gamma-ray Space Telescope studies gamma-ray sources in the universe, including pulsars, gamma-ray bursts, and active galactic nuclei.
- **Galactic Arm:** Regions of increased star formation and gas density within the disk of a spiral galaxy, often exhibiting spiral patterns.
- **Galactic Bulge:** The central, bulging region of a spiral galaxy, typically containing older stars and a high density of stars.
- **Galactic Disk:** The flattened, rotating component of a spiral galaxy, where most of the younger stars, gas, and dust is found.
- **Galactic Halo:** A spherical region surrounding the main disk of a galaxy, containing older stars, globular clusters, and dark matter.
- **Galactic Merger:** The process by which two or more galaxies collide and merge together, often triggering bursts of star formation and the formation of new structures.
- **Galactic Nucleus:** The central region of a galaxy, often containing a supermassive black hole and dense clusters of stars.
- **Galaxy Cluster:** A massive structure that consists of hundreds to thousands of galaxies bound together by gravity. They are among the largest known gravitationally bound structures in the universe.
- **Galaxy:** A large system of stars, gas, and dust bound together by gravity, typically containing millions or billions of stars.
- **GALEX (Galaxy Evolution Explorer):** Launched in 2003, GALEX observed the universe in ultraviolet wavelengths, studying the formation and evolution of galaxies.
- **Gamma-Ray Burst (GRB):** Some of the most energetic events in the universe, emitting intense bursts of gamma-ray radiation. They are brief and fleeting, typically lasting from a fraction of a second to a few minutes, but during this time, they can outshine entire galaxies.
- **Globular Cluster:** A spherical cluster of tens of thousands to hundreds of thousands of stars bound together by gravity, typically found in the halos of galaxies.
- **Gravitational Lensing:** A phenomenon predicted by Albert Einstein's theory of general relativity. It occurs when the gravitational field of a massive object, such as a galaxy or a cluster of galaxies, bends the light from a more distant object behind it. This bending of light can distort and magnify the appearance of the background object, effectively acting as a lens.
- **Great Attractor:** A gravitational anomaly in intergalactic space that is

drawing galaxies, including our Milky Way, towards it.

- **H II regions:** Clouds of ionized hydrogen found in interstellar space, typically associated with areas of active star formation, crucial for understanding the processes of stellar birth and the evolution of galaxies.
- **HARPS spectrograph:** An advanced instrument utilized in astronomy for the precise measurement of the radial velocities of stars.
- **Hawking Radiation:** A theoretical prediction in quantum mechanics, which suggests black holes emit radiation due to quantum effects near their event horizons.
- **Heliosphere:** A vast region of space around the Sun, where the solar wind, a stream of charged particles emanating from the Sun, interacts with the interstellar medium.
- **Hubble Space Telescope (HST):** Launched in 1990, the Hubble Space Telescope is one of the most well-known and beloved space telescopes. It has provided stunning images and groundbreaking scientific discoveries across a wide range of astronomical fields.
- **Inflation:** A period of extremely rapid expansion of the early universe, shortly after the Big Bang.
- **Interplanetary Medium:** The sparse collection of particles, fields, and radiation that exists in the vast regions of space between the bodies of the solar system.
- **Interstellar Medium (ISM):** The matter and radiation that exists in the space between the stars within a galaxy. It plays a crucial role in the formation and evolution of stars and galaxies, as well as in the dynamics of the interstellar environment.
- **Irregular Galaxy:** A type of galaxy that lacks a distinct regular shape, often exhibiting chaotic or asymmetric structures.
- **James Webb Space Telescope (JWST):** Scheduled for launch in 2022 (as of my last update), the James Webb Space Telescope is an upcoming flagship mission designed to be the successor to the Hubble Space Telescope. It will observe the universe in infrared wavelengths and is expected to revolutionize our understanding of the early universe, exoplanets, and more.
- **Kepler Space Telescope:** Launched in 2009, the Kepler Space Telescope was designed to search for exoplanets by monitoring the brightness of stars. It has discovered thousands of exoplanet candidates and confirmed many of them.

- **Kuiper Belt:** A region of the outer solar system beyond the orbit of Neptune that is populated with icy bodies, dwarf planets, and other small objects.
- **Light-Year:** A unit of distance used in astronomy to measure vast distances across space. It represents the distance that light travels in one year in a vacuum, approximately 9.46 trillion kilometers (or about 5.88 trillion miles). Since light travels at a finite speed, which is approximately 299,792 kilometers per second (or about 186,282 miles per second) in a vacuum, it takes about 1 year to traverse this immense distance. Light-years are commonly used to describe the distances between stars, galaxies, and other celestial objects, providing a convenient scale for understanding the immense size of the universe.
- **Local Group:** A galaxy group that includes the Milky Way and consists of over 50 galaxies bound together by gravity.
- **Lyman-alpha blobs (LABs):** Vast, luminous clouds of hydrogen gas that emit strongly in the Lyman-alpha spectral line. They are important objects of study in understanding the formation and evolution of galaxies in the early universe.
- **Magnetar:** A type of neutron star with an extremely powerful magnetic field, one of the most intense in the universe.
- **Magnetopause:** The boundary between a planet's magnetosphere and the surrounding solar wind or interplanetary magnetic field.
- **Magnetosphere:** The region of space surrounding a celestial body, such as a planet or a star, in which the motion of charged particles is influenced by its magnetic field.
- **NASA's Kepler Space Telescope:** A pioneering observatory designed to discover Earth-sized exoplanets orbiting other stars within our galaxy.
- **Near Infrared Camera (NIRCam) imaging:** One of the primary scientific instruments on the James Webb Space Telescope. It plays a crucial role in capturing detailed images of the universe in the near-infrared part of the spectrum.
- **Nebula:** An interstellar cloud of dust, hydrogen, helium, and other ionized gases where stars are born.
- **Neutrino:** Fundamental particles that belong to the family of leptons, which also includes electrons, muons, and tau particles.
- **Neutron Star:** One of the possible end states of a massive star after a supernova explosion. It is an extremely dense and compact object primarily composed of neutrons, hence the name.

- **New General Catalogue of Nebulae and Clusters of Stars(NGC):** An astronomical catalogue of deep-sky objects compiled by John Louis Emil Dreyer in 1888. The NGC contains 7,840 objects, including galaxies, star clusters and emission nebulae.
- **NuSTAR (Nuclear Spectroscopic Telescope Array):** Launched in 2012, NuSTAR is the first telescope capable of focusing high-energy X-rays. It has been used to study black holes, supernovae remnants, and other energetic phenomena.
- **Observable Universe:** The portion of the universe that can be seen from Earth, limited by the speed of light and the age of the universe.
- **Oort Cloud:** The Oort Cloud is a hypothetical region of space surrounding the Sun, extending far beyond the Kuiper Belt, and is believed to be the source of long-period comets.
- **Parsec (pc):** A unit of distance used in astronomy to measure large distances beyond the solar system. The term "parsec" is a contraction of "parallax of one arcsecond," and it is defined as the distance at which one astronomical unit (AU) subtends an angle of one arcsecond.
- **Planet:** A celestial body that orbits a star, is spherical in shape due to its own gravity, and has cleared its orbit of other debris.
- **Planetary Nebula:** An astronomical phenomenon that represents a short-lived phase in the life cycle of intermediate-mass stars.
- **Population II stars:** Population II stars formed after the first generation of stars (Population III stars), which were composed almost entirely of hydrogen and helium produced in the Big Bang. Population III stars synthesized heavier elements through nucleosynthesis and dispersed them into the interstellar medium through supernovae, from which Population II stars subsequently formed.
- **Pulsar:** A highly magnetized, rotating neutron star that emits beams of electromagnetic radiation from its magnetic poles. These beams of radiation sweep across space like the beams of a lighthouse as the pulsar rotate, leading to regular pulses of radiation observed on Earth.
- **Quasar:** A highly energetic and distant active galactic nucleus powered by a supermassive black hole.
- **Radial velocity method:** Also known as the Doppler spectroscopy method, is a technique used to detect exoplanets by observing the motion of a star as it is influenced by the gravitational pull of an orbiting planet.
- **Redshift:** The phenomenon where light from distant objects is shifted

towards longer (redder) wavelengths due to the expansion of the universe.

- **Sloan Digital Sky Survey (SDSS):** A comprehensive astronomical survey that maps the sky in multiple wavelengths of light. It has provided extensive data on millions of celestial objects, including stars, galaxies, and quasars, facilitating research across various fields of astronomy.
- **Spiral Galaxy:** A type of galaxy characterized by a flat, rotating disk with spiral arms and a central bulge, such as the Milky Way.
- **Spitzer Space Telescope:** Launched in 2003, the Spitzer Space Telescope observes the universe in the infrared spectrum. It has contributed to our understanding of star formation, exoplanets, and the composition of distant galaxies.
- **Star:** A luminous sphere of plasma held together by its own gravity, undergoing nuclear fusion in its core.
- **Subaru Telescope and the Keck Observatory:** Two of the world's leading astronomical observatories located on Mauna Kea, Hawaii.
- **Supercluster Complex:** A large-scale structure in the universe consisting of multiple galaxy clusters and groups gravitationally bound to one another. These structures are among the largest known in the universe, spanning hundreds of millions of light-years across.
- **Supermassive Black Hole:** An extremely massive black hole typically found at the center of galaxies, with a mass millions to billions of times that of the Sun.
- **Supernova:** The explosive death of a massive star, resulting in a burst of radiation and the creation of heavy elements.
- **TESS (Transiting Exoplanet Survey Satellite):** Launched in 2018, TESS is a space telescope designed to search for exoplanets using the transit method. It has already discovered thousands of exoplanet candidates and confirmed many of them.
- **Tidal Interaction:** Gravitational interactions between galaxies that can distort their shapes, trigger star formation, and lead to the exchange of material.
- **Time travel:** A concept in physics and science fiction that refers to the hypothetical ability to move backward or forward in time, either within one's own timeline or to a different point in history or the future.
- **Transiting Exoplanet Survey Satellite (TESS):** A space telescope designed and operated by NASA with the primary mission of discovering exoplanets orbiting bright stars in the solar neighborhood.

- **Very Large Array (VLA) radio telescope:** One of the world's premier radio astronomy observatories, located on the Plains of San Agustin in New Mexico, USA. VLA consists of 27 individual radio antennas, each of which has a dish diameter of 25 meters. The VLA operates over a wide range of radio frequencies, from 1 GHz to 50 GHz.
- **Virgo Supercluster:** Also known as the Local Supercluster, is a massive cluster of galaxy clusters that includes the Local Group, to which our Milky Way galaxy belongs.
- **Void:** A vast, largely empty region of space with very few galaxies, stars, or other forms of matter.
- **White Dwarf:** A small, dense star that represents the final evolutionary stage of stars not massive enough to become neutron stars or black holes.
- **XMM-Newton:** Launched in 1999, XMM-Newton is an X-ray observatory operated by the European Space Agency (ESA). It has provided valuable data on topics such as black holes, galaxy clusters, and the interstellar medium.
- **Zodiacal Light:** Zodiacal light is a faint, diffuse, and roughly triangular-shaped glow seen in the night sky, caused by sunlight scattering off interplanetary dust particles in the solar system.

Appendix 1: Life Cycle Of A Star

The life cycle of a star begins when the gravitational collapse occurs within a nebula (interstellar cloud of dust and gas), which mainly involves hydrogen molecules. The concentration progressively heats up and forms a Protostar which initially emits infrared light. Eventually, the temperature of the core rises and the new born start emitting visible light. This phase takes place for around thousands to millions of years, depending on the mass of the Protostar.

As the core becomes hotter, nuclear fusion of hydrogen atoms takes place. Hydrogen nuclei collide and fuse into helium, releasing vast amount of energy. This energy is propagated through convection and radiation to the outer layers of the stars thus counterbalancing the gravitational force. The rate of fusion depends on the star's mass, with more massive stars burning fuel at a faster rate than less massive ones.

As the core runs out of hydrogen, the balance between gravity and radiation pressure is disrupted, leading to changes in the star's structure and behavior. Once the nuclear fusion stops, the core stars contracting because the pressure from the outer layers. This results in the heating up of the core, allowing hydrogen fusion in the outer layers. This process continues and produces heavier elements like carbon and oxygen. This eventually turns a star into a Red Giant or a Super Giant.

When a massive star finishes its fusion process and is unable to counteract gravitational forces, it experiences a dramatic collapse, leading to a supernova explosion. This phenomenon emits a tremendous amount of energy, outshining entire galaxies and scattering heavy elements throughout space.

Depending on the star's mass, the leftovers of a supernova explosion can become either a neutron star or a black hole. Neutron stars are extremely dense entities made almost entirely of neutrons, whereas black holes are areas of spacetime with such intense gravity that nothing, including light, can escape from them.

The material ejected during a supernova explosion enriches the surrounding interstellar medium with heavy elements, which can then become the building blocks for new stars, planets, and life.

Appendix 2: Type Of Star Based On Temperature

On the basis of surface temperature of the star, they can be classified into seven types using spectral classification system.

1. O-type: Hot blue star with surface temperature around 10,000-30,000 K. It is extremely luminous and massive, exhibiting strong ionized helium lines and weaker hydrogen lines in their spectra. These stars have short lifespan.
2. B-type: Large and luminous blue-white stars having temperatures in range 10,000 K to 25,000 K, with spectral lines of strong hydrogen, neutral helium and singly ionized metals.
3. A-type: White stars with their mass between 1.4 and 2.1 solar masses and surface temperature of 7,500-10,000 K. These stars have strong hydrogen lines and ionized metals lines with shorter lifespan than the Sun.
4. F-type: Yellow-white stars having surface temperature around 6000-7500 K with weaker hydrogen lines and strong ionized metal lines. Their mass is slightly more mass and higher luminosity than the Sun.
5. G-type: Yellow stars with size and luminosity similar to the Sun. They exhibit lines of ionized calcium and other metals and surface temperature of 5,200 to 6,000 K
6. K-type: Orange stars which are cooler and less luminous the Sun, with strong lines of neutral metals like iron, calcium, and titanium. They have longer lifespan.
7. M-type: Red stars having surface temperature around 2,400-3,700 K. They are coolest and least luminous stars, with strong molecular bands, particularly titanium oxide (TiO). They have very long lifespan.

Appendix 3: Further Read

- Kuiper Gerard P., Middlehurst Barbara M. 1975. Galaxies and the universe, University of Chicago Press; ISBN 13: 9780226459615
- Nicholas E White, Alphonso V Diaz. 2004. Beyond Einstein: from the Big Bang to black holes. NASA Goddard Space Flight Center, Greenbelt, MD 20771, USA Advances in Space Research, Elsevier; Volume 34, Issue 3, Pages 651-658
- Paul Halpern. 2012. Edge of the Universe: A Voyage to the Cosmic Horizon and Beyond. John Wiley & Sons; ISBN13: 978-0470636244
- New Scientist. 2018. A Journey Through The Universe: A traveler's guide from the centre of the sun to the edge of the unknown, John Murray Learning
- Beryl E Clotfelter. 1976. The universe and its structure, McGraw-Hill; ISBN13: 978-0070113855
- George B. Field.1978.Cosmic Evolution: Introduction to Astronomy, Houghton Mifflin; ISBN13: 978-0395253212
- Jerry B. Marion. 1970. A Universe of Physics: A Book of Readings, John Wiley & Sons; ISBN13: 978-0471569138
- Carl Sagan. 2002. Cosmos, Random House; ISBN13: 9780375508325
- Igor D. Novikov. 1983. Evolution of the Universe, Cambridge University Press; ISBN13: 978-0521241298
- Narlikar, J. V. 2002. An Introduction to Cosmology, Cambridge University Press; ISBN13: 978-0521793766
- A.Karel Velan. 1992. The Multi-universe Cosmos: First Complete Story of the Origin of the Universe, Kluwer Academic / Plenum Publishers; ISBN13: 978-0306442674
- Narlikar, J. V. 1996. Elements of Cosmology Paperback – 1 January 1996, Universities Press; ISBN13: 978-8173710438